Deuteronomy

Langham

PREACHING RESOURCES

Deuteronomy

The God Who Keeps Promises

Paul Barker

Langham

PREACHING RESOURCES

© 2017 by Paul Barker

Published 2017 by Langham Preaching Resources
an imprint of Langham Creative Projects

Langham Partnership
PO Box 296, Carlisle, Cumbria CA3 9WZ, UK
www.langham.org

First published by Pustaka SUFES, in Malaysia in 2011.

ISBNs:
978-1-78368-122-8 Print
978-1-78368-153-2 Mobi
978-1-78368-152-5 ePub
978-1-78368-154-9 PDF

British Library Cataloguing in Publication Data
A catalogue record for this book is available from the British Library

ISBN: 978-1-78368-122-8

Cover & Book Design: projectluz.com

Contents

Preface

This book is written with the firm conviction that the Old Testament, and not least the book of Deuteronomy, ought to be taken seriously by modern Christians. In particular, in Deuteronomy we discover the rich theology of the God who keeps promises, for Deuteronomy is a book which encourages and persuades us to trust in a faithful God. It is my hope that this book instils in its readers a greater trust in that same God.

This book began life as a series of talks for an Australian Fellowship of Evangelical Students conference in 1991 though the bulk of the material was honed in preaching a series of sermons on Deuteronomy in two wonderful congregations: St Matthew's Cheltenham, England, who supported me so lovingly during my doctoral study sojourn in a strange land, and Holy Trinity Doncaster, Melbourne, whom it was an honour and privilege to serve as Senior Minister from April 1996 to November 2009. I thank God enormously for both congregations. The first edition of this book was published by Acorn Press, Melbourne, and was dedicated to these two congregations with the prayer that they may continue to fear the Lord, walk in all his ways, love him and serve him with all their heart and soul (Deut 10:12).

This book was then republished in 2011 in Malaysia, where I have lived since 2009 by Pustaka SUFES, and was dedicated to my students at Seminari Theoloji Malaysia with the same prayer as above.

Now it is being republished with some minor revisions by Langham Preaching Resources in order to be made more widely available, and not least for preachers. We have slightly modified the "Questions for Discussion," added an appendix on Preaching Deuteronomy, modified the footnotes, and made a few other minor changes. At the time of writing, I am the Regional Coordinator for Langham Preaching Asia, and I am delighted to have this privilege to contribute to the growth of biblical preaching in the world, to encourage preaching to be more faithful, clear and relevant, and preachers to be more godly in character. This edition is dedicated to those whom Langham Preaching is training throughout the world.

Paul Barker
February 2016

Introduction

I first read the book of Deuteronomy when I was a university student. I had decided to read through the entire Bible. After ploughing tediously through Leviticus and Numbers, I resolved to use a long train trip from Melbourne to Sydney to get this next book out of the way. My perseverance paid dividends. This was not tedious or dull; Deuteronomy was riveting stuff! I was engrossed and took notes of some of the wonderful verses I read. Sadly, all too many people think Deuteronomy is a difficult, legal and cultic book with little relevance today. If that is you, you are wrong!

Deuteronomy is primarily a sermon. "These are the words that Moses spoke" (Deut 1:1). Not only is this apparent from the form of the book, it is also clear from its style. The form of the book is almost entirely speech. Apart from chapter 34, there are only about five other major paragraphs in the book which are not reported speech. This is especially clear in the RSV where virtually every paragraph begins with quotation marks (unfortunately the NRSV does not put in all these quotation marks).

The Story So Far: Genesis – Numbers

The occasion for Moses' words is the eve of Israel entering the land of Canaan, to the west of the Jordan River, a land promised by God centuries before to Abraham (Gen 12:1; 15:7). Those promises have been the guiding theme in the books of Genesis, Exodus, Leviticus and Numbers. Though there are long passages of laws, especially in Exodus and Leviticus, the storyline has concerned the working out of the promises to Abraham.

In Genesis 12–50, God keeps his promises to provide children for Abraham. These chapters deal with four generations: Abraham, his son Isaac, his son Jacob, and his twelve sons, the most prominent being Joseph. However, Genesis ends with this extended family in Egypt, away from the land God had promised. Does the promise still stand?

The book of Exodus takes up the story four hundred years later. Still in Egypt, still away from the Promised Land, the descendants of Abraham have become numerous, as God promised, but are now slaves. In answer to the people's cries, and because of his promises to Abraham, God acts to rescue the Israelites from Egypt (Exod 2:23–25).

He raises up a man called Moses to lead Israel. Through various miracles of God performed against the Egyptian king (Pharaoh) and people, God enables the Israelites to flee through the parted Red Sea (Exod 3–15). Between Egypt and Israel is desert. The Israelites come to Mt Sinai where God speaks to them and gives them the Ten Commandments (Exod 19–20) and many other laws (Exod 21–40; Lev).

The Israelites then set out towards the Promised Land (Num 10) but do not enter it because of fear of the inhabitants (Num 13–14). As punishment, God condemns the people to spend forty years in the desert while the adult generation dies and the next generation is given the task of entering the Promised Land. At the end of that forty-year period, Israel travels again towards the land, this time towards the east. It is here, overlooking the land in the Plains of Moab, that Moses, now an old man, speaks the words of Deuteronomy.

At this significant time in Israel's history, Moses preaches. He is about to die and chapter 34 reports his death. Yet Deuteronomy is more than a farewell speech. It is a full-blown sermon, urging, pleading and exhorting the Israelites to live faithfully and obediently in this land. This stirring sermon climaxes in the appeal for the Israelites to "choose life" (Deut 30:19).

Deuteronomy: A Sermon

The style of the book of Deuteronomy is sermonic. There is a ringing call to action and a strong sense of urgency. Laws are preached, not merely repeated or listed. Moses is urging obedience to the law and not just detailing what the law requires. As we are told in Deuteronomy 1:5, "Moses undertook to expound this law as follows" (to expound is to make clear). The same word is used in 27:8. So Deuteronomy is not strictly a repeat of the law given firstly in the book of Exodus on Mount Sinai (see Exod 19–24 for this account). Rather, Deuteronomy presupposes knowledge of the laws already given and devotes its attention to preaching, exhorting and motivating Israel to obey them (e.g. 14:22–27; 15:1–11). Instead of "this is what you must do," Deuteronomy says, "Do it."

Deuteronomy, then, is thoroughly rhetorical, consistent with its origin being a spoken word rather than a written word. Rhetorical devices abound, being used to motivate and stir up the hearers to love and obedience. For example, the land, a major focus of the book, is almost invariably qualified by terms such as "which the Lord your God gave you," "the good," "flowing with milk and honey" and "which the Lord your God swore (or promised) to give you." These constantly repeated expressions are to give Israel confidence in God's faithfulness to his promises and to make Israel eager to take the land because it is so good and prosperous. Almost every time Moses talks about the land, he wants to motivate Israel.

In a similar way, the key imperatives to love, fear, serve, obey, walk after and hold fast, and others, keep recurring as an integral part of this exhortation (e.g. 6:13; 10:12ff.; 13:4; etc.). They are general terms summing up how Israel is to properly respond to God. They have overlapping senses so that when one or two of these imperatives occur we call to mind the others. This can be seen from the fact that the expression "with all your heart, and with all your soul" is attached in different places to different words (compare 4:29; 6:5; 10:12; etc.).

The importance of noting that Deuteronomy is a sermon is that this makes clear the function of the book. The form and style of a book in the Bible often suggests its function. This is the case with Deuteronomy which has the function of eliciting a response of faith and obedience on the part of Israel as they set out to conquer the land.

Moses' sermon worked. That is, after his death, and under the leadership of his successor Joshua, Israel entered the land and defeated the inhabitants. This is recounted in the book of Joshua. Israel's subsequent history is continued in Judges and the books of Samuel and Kings. These take the story of Israel up to 560 BC.

The Origins of Deuteronomy

Traditionally, Jews and Christians have attributed the book of Deuteronomy to Moses, some even going so far as to say he wrote the account of his own death in chapter 34. Over the last century there has been a general consensus among scholars that the book was written much later. Many associate Deuteronomy with the book of the law found in the temple in about 622 BC in the time of King Josiah (see 2 Kgs 22). Though the response of Josiah to the finding of this book does suggest a relationship to Deuteronomy, this does not necessarily imply the book was written then and "planted" in the temple in order to be found.

This is not the place to argue in detail the dating and authorship of the book. Many of the commentaries referred to at the end of this book do that quite adequately. Certainly Deuteronomy itself claims to be written in large part by Moses (e.g. 31:24–29). Some scholars suggest this only means the laws and not the opening and closing chapters. However, it seems to me that the book has a greater unity encompassing all its chapters. Thus we acknowledge that Deuteronomy is faithful to Moses even if there are some later additions such as the final chapter.

The Structure of the Book

Many scholars make a point about the structure of Deuteronomy, arguing that it reflects various ancient covenant agreements or treaties. Depending on what they consider Deuteronomy to most closely resemble, they attach a corresponding date to the book.

One of the dangers of this approach is that it fails to recognize that primarily Deuteronomy is a sermon, a spoken word, and not, originally, a document. It does not rigidly conform in every detail to an ancient covenant document though there are obviously some parallels.[1] For example, ancient covenant documents would simply list the requirements that the weaker partner was obliged to fulfil. In Deuteronomy, there is exhortation to keep such requirements rather than a straightforward enumeration of them. The parallels include aspects such as having some account of previous history at the beginning, instructions about the ongoing maintenance of the relationship and witnesses to its agreement.

Where the scholarly discussion in recent years has been helpful is in trying to pinpoint the nature of the relationship between God and his people Israel. At its heart this relationship of course is personal and depends on God, rather than being merely documentary, depending on a treaty. However, Deuteronomy is above all about an important relationship, between the one, true, living God of the Bible and his people.

It is helpful to note the following major sections in the book:

Ch 1–4   Introduction, historical survey, exhortation
Ch 5–11   General call to faith and obedience

---

1. There are three major positions in this argument. (1) Deuteronomy reflects ancient Hittite treaties made between a suzerain and his vassals. This view suggests a date roughly contemporary with Moses in the 13th to 15th centuries BC. (2) Deuteronomy reflects Assyrian treaties, dated approximately 700 BC; (3) The Old Testament covenant form, as reflected in Deuteronomy, is distinctive and not exactly like any other Ancient Near Eastern treaties. See J. A. Thompson, *Deuteronomy* (TOTC; London: IVP, 1974) 17–21, 47–68.

Ch 12–26	Exhortation to keep specific laws
Ch 27–28	Blessings and curses of the covenant
Ch 29–30	The challenge to keep the covenant
Ch 31–33	Passing on the covenant to the next generation
Ch 34	Death of Moses

The Value of Deuteronomy Today

The response Moses called for was a response not to a sermon, nor to the preacher, nor to a particular situation, nor to various laws, but was, fundamentally, a response to a gracious God who had acted to save and had made promises about his continuing relationship with Israel. The priority lies with God's action and grace. In response to this God, two things are called for: faith in the promises of God and trusting God to keep them, and obedience to his standards and laws. The two essentially go together. Thus the structure that is crucial is not a treaty structure but a theological structure. The reader needs to keep this big picture in mind when reading Deuteronomy in order to see this pattern undergirding individual passages.

For the Christian today, this framework is also significant. It is the same sort of framework as, for example, we find in Ephesians or Romans or some sermons in Acts. God has acted in grace to establish by redemption a people for himself who, in turn, are called to respond in certain ways to that God. This consistency reminds us that the God of Deuteronomy, and the Old Testament in general, is the same God of the New Testament. The response God requires of the Christian is, in broad terms, that required of Israel in Deuteronomy, namely faith and obedience.

Herein lies some of the abiding value and worth of studying the book of Deuteronomy today. God wants our trust and faith as we respond to his grace, faithfulness and promises. He also requires our obedience to his laws, that his people may "lead a life worthy of the calling to which you have been called" (Eph 4:1). Preachers and ministers today who wish to accurately preach the Bible will do well by keeping this framework in mind in their sermons, learning from this great example by Moses.

There are some obvious problems for the Christian in dealing with Deuteronomy and applying it to contemporary times. Deuteronomy urges the complete destruction, without mercy, of the inhabitants of Canaan. Many Christians recoil from such warfare and apparent bloodthirstiness, and rightly so. Yet rather than throwing out the whole book as being outdated and no longer relevant, we find the underlying principles to be significant. Our approach to Old Testament laws in this book is to determine the theological and ethical principles behind each law, recognizing that in Deuteronomy laws are a combination of general principles and specific applications. The Christian's task is to reapply those same principles in his or her own situation, recognizing that some principles are modified in the light of the New Testament and others remain abiding. For this approach in practice, see the body of this book.

In all the Old Testament, Deuteronomy holds a special place in calling for a heartfelt, inner faith as it stirs up in its hearers and readers a right spirit and attitude to God. Moses preached because the Israelites needed God's word, needed to remember God's acts and promises and needed their hearts softened to respond. In the same way, we need God's word, need to remember God's acts and promises and need our hearts softened. It is easy to forget. It is easy to have a hard heart. "What does the Lord your God require of you? Only to fear the Lord your God, to walk in all his ways, to love him, to serve the Lord your God with all your heart and with all your soul, and to keep the commandments of the Lord your God." (Deut 10:12–13). Whenever we read and study the Bible it is good to pray, to ask God to open our minds to understand his word and to open our hearts to obey it.

1

Learning from the Past

As a child I loved learning history. I have a good mind for dates and insignificant details and used to know the dates of all the kings and queens of England since 1066. However, this sort of learning history was, by and large, an accumulation of knowledge.

Learning history for the sake of the present is a different matter. It is said that the only thing we learn from history is that we learn nothing from history. Lessons of the past are lost and all too often only relearned after the same mistakes have been made again.

Deuteronomy begins with a history lesson but not merely for the sake of accumulation of knowledge. While Moses recounts some incidents of Israel's past forty years in the wilderness, it is not to give a record of what happened. That is recorded in Exodus, Leviticus and Numbers. Only selected incidents are mentioned here. What Moses has done is to choose some events of Israel's past in order to make some important points to Israel about the present and future. We need to ask why these events are recorded and what lessons are being taught.

Where to Start?

Noting that Moses has been selective about which events of Israel's history he has included is important. The process of selection indicates purpose. Why didn't Moses begin at the original Passover and Exodus? Surely that is the ideal starting point? Nearly forty years before the time of this sermon in Deuteronomy, God raised up Moses, with his brother Aaron, to lead the Israelites out of Egypt to this promised land (see Exod 1–19). At that time the people of Israel was largely enslaved to the Egyptians. Moses and Aaron negotiated with the Pharaoh of Egypt for the people to be released. They performed many miracles but it was only when the firstborn of all the

Egyptians were killed that Pharaoh finally relented long enough for Israel to leave quickly. That final night, Israel's own firstborn were spared, or passed over, because the Israelites had put blood on their doorposts as commanded (Exod 12:1–28). This was the great act of Old Testament redemption, the highlight of Israel's salvation. Yet strikingly Moses does not start his historical recall here.

Instead, he begins by mentioning the command of God to leave Mt Sinai:

> The Lord your God spoke to us at Horeb, saying, "You have stayed
> long enough at this mountain. Resume your journey, and go into
> the hill country of the Amorites as well as into the neighbouring
> regions – the Arabah, the hill country, the Shephelah, the Negeb,
> and the seacoast – the land of the Canaanites and the Lebanon,
> as far as the great river, the river Euphrates. See, I have set the
> land before you; go in and take possession of the land that I
> swore to your ancestors, to Abraham, to Isaac and to Jacob, to
> give to them and to their descendants after them." (Deut 1:6–8)

Why? It is because the focus of Moses' exhortation throughout Deuteronomy is land, not liberation. The liberation of Israel from Egypt is a past event now accomplished. It is not to be forgotten (e.g. 26:5–9), but nonetheless it is not now Moses' primary concern. In the Plains of Moab, overlooking the Jordan River, and on the eve of crossing over under Moses' successor, Joshua, land and its possession is the crucial issue.

The God Who Keeps Promises (1:1–18)

So Moses begins at Mount Sinai, usually called Horeb in Deuteronomy. Mount Horeb is where God gave Israel the law, including the Ten Commandments. Israel was there just a few weeks after leaving Egypt. It was there that Israel turned its focus towards the Promised Land. Thus 1:7 spells out in detail the area of land given to Israel. Mostly these areas run north to south in strips, the description going from east to west. The Arabah is the Jordan valley and the valley around the Dead Sea. The hill country is the next strip of land westward from the Jordan. It is rugged, steep and, for much of it, a wilderness area. The Shephelah is the name for the lower, more undulating foothills west of the hill country. The seacoast refers to the strip of flat plain area along the Mediterranean Sea. Finally, the Negeb is the desert to the south of

Israel. All this land is Canaanite land. The Lebanon is to the north, as is the river Euphrates.

This is the land of promise, promised to Abraham, Isaac and Jacob (1:8). It is where Abram and Sarai went in Genesis 12:5. A crucial feature of Deuteronomy is illustrated here. Land "sworn to your ancestors" is a recurring theme (e.g. 1:35; 6:10, 18, 23; 7:13; 8:1; 9:5; 10:11; etc.). It is not any land that Israel is about to enter. It is promised land. It is sworn land. God, indeed Yahweh, the covenant name for God (1:6; see Exod 3 for the explanation of this name), has promised this land. This appeal to Yahweh's promise is meant to encourage Israel to enter and conquer the land. The dilemma is, can God's promise be trusted?

This question governs the selection of events of Israel's past history in 1:9 to 3:29 and is answered affirmatively. The recital of past history demonstrates God's faithfulness. God's promise of land can be trusted. We know this because of the way God has acted in the recent past.

The incident recalled in 1:9–18 refers back to Exodus 18:13–27. Why does Moses bother to recall the appointment of assistants to lead and judge the tribes? This episode seems to have nothing to do with the possession of the land. Why is it included in this historical overview? The purpose behind this being included seems to be that the need for delegated authority is a clear demonstration that Yahweh has indeed been keeping his promise. Land was not the only promise God made to Abram. Another key aspect of the promises to Abram in Genesis 12:2–3 was for descendants. As well, in Genesis 15:5, God said to Abram, "Look toward heaven and count the stars, if you are able to count them. So shall your descendants be." What has Moses said in Deuteronomy 1:10? "The LORD your God has multiplied you, so that today you are as numerous as the stars of heaven." The promise to Abram in Genesis is fulfilled. Moses uses the same expression about the stars in the sky to make this clear. It is a deliberate reference back to the promise of Genesis 15. The appointment of assistants also supports this point. The need for assistants for Moses is proof that the people have become extremely numerous. There is no doubt at all. God is faithful. Part of the covenant to Abram has been fulfilled. The Israelites can look around and see for themselves. They are a numerous people.

Interestingly, Moses acknowledges in 1:11 that there is more to come. Yes the promise is fulfilled, but God will bring even more descendants. God's character is such that he always seeks fulfilment in overflowing ways. He is not a God who holds back in his faithfulness and generosity.

The implication of what Moses is driving at should be obvious. If God has been faithful in fulfilling just a part of the covenant promises to Abram, then he can be trusted to fulfil the rest also. He is a covenant-keeping, promise-keeping God. He can be trusted. Here in Moab, after forty years in the wilderness, and with Moses himself about to die, God can be trusted. What encouragement for Israel at this crucial time. God will not let them down.

Israel in the Wilderness

The characteristic picture of Israel in the wilderness is of a nation wandering aimlessly, blundering on from mistake to mistake. This picture is not entirely accurate. Even in the wilderness, Israel, at times, is a model of obedience and not just failure. In 1:19, Israel goes from Horeb (Sinai) to Kadesh-barnea, "just as the Lord our God had ordered us." In that one verse Israel moves from the far south, Horeb, to much further north, well on the way to the land of promise. Now look at verse 46 and see where Israel is. Still at Kadesh-barnea! In 2:1, Israel is going backwards into the wilderness, away from the land of promise.

As Israel obeys, it goes towards its goal, realizing God's promise. As it disobeys, it goes away, or at best remains stationary. Israel's obedience is to be a means of bringing about the fulfilment of God's promises. Israel is not to sit down and await God's fulfilment but is to be the means for bringing that about. Israel is therefore to co-operate with God in bringing about his purposes.

Though 1:19 simply recounts an episode of obedience, the focus of the rest of chapter 1 is on a stationary Israel in Kadesh (1:20–46). Moses gives this incident a great deal of attention because it is so important for teaching a crucial lesson. Israel at Kadesh is essentially in the same position as the next generation in the Plains of Moab forty years later, now being addressed by Moses in Deuteronomy. Though Kadesh is to the south of the Promised Land and the Plains of Moab are to the east, both are on the border. Moses is most concerned to see that Israel does not repeat the mistakes of Kadesh, for if it does, the people may well be back in the wilderness for yet another generation.

Israel's Failure (1:19–46)

It is worth looking more closely at Israel's mistakes at Kadesh. They are twofold. First, Israel lacks faith. Lacking faith, the people request spies to check the land. They are afraid of the inhabitants: "Our kindred have made our hearts melt by reporting, 'The people are stronger and taller than we, the cities are large and fortified up to heaven!'" (1:28). Moses' summary is in verse 32, "you have no trust in the Lord your God." Israel lacked faith. It feared the Canaanites rather than God. It didn't trust in God's promises or his ability to fulfil them.

Second, Israel disobeyed. "You were unwilling to go up. You rebelled against the command of the LORD your God" (1:26). Lack of faith is seen in disobedience. The two go hand in hand. Indeed, one is impossible without the other. You cannot obey God without faith. You cannot have faith without demonstrating obedience. Though an oversimplification, it is true that God gives promises which call for faith and trust and he gives commands, calling for obedience, which in part are the means of fulfilling the promises. God's promises are freely and graciously pledged. The fulfilment of them calls for an active response. For Israel in Deuteronomy the key promise is that of land, promised to Abraham hundreds of years before. The fulfilment of this promise calls for Israel's active response in faith and obedience. There can be no conquest without this.

The same pattern is found in the New Testament. The glorious promises of God of eternal life and blessing are freely made to us. Yet God calls us to appropriate these promises with both faith and obedience. There is a danger if Christians think falsely that faith is intellectual or internal only. That is not the faith the Bible commends. Biblical faith is always active in obedience.

Hebrews 11, for example, shows this clearly. That is the case most definitely in Deuteronomy too. In the example of 1:19–46, Israel's lack of faith is actually disobedience because it refuses to go in and enter the land.

This is what Moses is getting at in these opening chapters of Deuteronomy. He wants to stir up faith because faith produces obedience. If Israel is to obey the command to take the land, then it must have faith in God. What stimulates faith is remembering the faithfulness of God to his promises. Thus we have an appeal to an essential characteristic of God. So, deep in the heart of this section recounting Israel's disobedience at Kadesh is the striking affirmation: "It is a good land that the Lord our God is giving us" (1:25). As if God could be doubted! Believe it, Moses is saying. It is true. It is a good land. God promised as much; the spies testify to it. You have no need to be frightened, for God is faithful. Tragically the previous generation disbelieved and disobeyed. Their failure is shown to be all the more culpable, and their excuses in verse 28 groundless, given the unequivocally positive report of the land by the spies in verse 25. Note that in Numbers 13:28 the spies themselves express fear of the inhabitants. Moses' further encouragement is also unheeded. He says,

> Have no dread or fear of them. The Lord your God, who goes before you, is the one who will fight for you, just as he did for you in Egypt before your very eyes, and in the wilderness, where you saw how the Lord your God carried you, just as one carries a child, all the way that you travelled until you reached this place. (1:29-31)

The people did not listen. Note the beginning of verses 26 and 32, "But . . ." Despite the spies' words and Moses' words, Israel rebels. It has no excuse.

Having refused to enter the land of promise, now Israel refuses to go back into the wilderness (1:43). Pig-headed, insolent, trusting in itself and not God, Israel attacks, but is soundly beaten back (1:44). Note that Amorite in verse 44 is a general term for the inhabitants of the land and, here, is largely synonymous with Canaanite. Then we read: "When you returned and wept before the Lord, the Lord would neither heed your voice nor pay you any attention" (1:45). The withdrawal or absence of God is a severe punishment which lasted for nearly forty years, yet in God's grace he continued to provide, protect and to care (2:7). God's punishment was for this generation of Israelites to die out before the land was taken by their children. The exceptions were to be Caleb and Joshua (1:36, 38). A journey which should have taken a matter of weeks took forty years (1:2, 3). Yet, despite his righteous punishment, there is always a future with God.

This episode at Kadesh serves as a severe warning to this next generation who, in similar circumstances, face similar temptations. Israel at Kadesh typifies humanity's natural tendency to unbelief and disobedience. Lack of faith is always equated with rebellion against God. Israel in the Plains of Moab must now learn the lessons of the past.

Israel's Progress (2:1–2:25)

From 2:1 to 3:11, Moses recalls Israel's dealings with Edom, Moab, Ammon, Sihon and Og, five nations to the south and east of the Promised Land. This recollection is, for Moses and his hearers, recent history, personally experienced by most of this current generation. It is retold therefore, not to make Israel aware of what happened but to learn from what happened. Again Moses is selective. Much is passed over in 2:1, about thirty-eight years of history. Surprisingly, Israel's encounters with these five nations show that Israel is now obeying and believing. What lessons are being taught here?

First, these episodes demonstrate again the faithfulness of God. He is not merely the God of Israel, but God of all the nations. He gives land to whomever he wills and, having given it, protects it. It is God who gave Mt Seir to Esau and Edom "as a possession" (2:5). It is God who gave Ar to Lot and Moab "as a possession" (2:9). It is God who gave land to Ammon "as a possession" (2:19). As a result, God protects these nations and their land, even from Israel. Edom is descended from Esau, Jacob's brother (Gen 25:30; 36:1), Moab and Ammon from Lot, Abraham's nephew (Gen 19:36–38). These three countries lay to the southeast of Canaan, roughly alongside the Dead Sea. In the same way, God is giving land to Israel "as a possession" (2:12).[1] Israel is urged to see the significance of its peaceful encounters with Edom, Moab and Ammon on their way north. For just as God had given and protected the land for those nations, so will he do for Israel. God can be trusted. He is God over the nations and able to keep his promises. Moses is stirring up Israel to trust God. He is trustworthy!

The second lesson goes with the first: God is able. Trustworthiness without ability is useless. Imagine you promise to meet a friend at a certain time. If you are not a trustworthy person, your friend will not believe your promise. And even if you are trustworthy, you may not keep your promise since circumstances beyond your control may prevent you. Not only do you need to be trustworthy; you also need to be able to keep the promise. In these chapters Moses is demonstrating that God is both trustworthy and able to keep his promises. There are no circumstances beyond God's ability or power.

Take a look at 2:10–12 and 20–23. These little asides are often overlooked. They look rather dull being full of strange names.

> The Emim – a large and numerous people, as tall as the Anakim – had formerly inhabited it. Like the Anakim, they are usually reckoned as Rephaim, though the Moabites call them Emim. Moreover, the Horim had formerly inhabited Seir, but the descendants of Esau dispossessed them, destroying them and settling in their place, as Israel had done in the land that the Lord gave them as a possession. . . .

---

1. The identical expression, an uncommon one, is used to stress the parallel between Israel and the other nations here.

It is usually reckoned as a land of Rephaim. Rephaim formerly inhabited it, though the Ammonites call them Zamzummim, a strong and numerous people, as tall as the Anakim. But the Lord destroyed them from before the Ammonites so that they could dispossess them and settle in their place. He did the same for the descendants of Esau, who live in Seir, by destroying the Horim before them so that they could dispossess them and settle in their place even to this day. As for the Avvim, who had lived in settlements in the vicinity of Gaza, the Caphtorim, who came from Caphtor, destroyed them and settled in their place.

These verses serve an important function. They emphasize that it is God's prerogative to move nations around. The two incidents recorded here involve two powerful, numerous and large, giant-like nations who are defeated under God's sovereignty. Do you remember Israel's fear at Kadesh in 1:28? "The people are stronger and taller than we . . . We actually saw there the offspring of the Anakim!" (see vv. 11 and 21). The Anakim are mentioned again. These asides are directly addressing Israel's fear expressed at Kadesh. Israel is concerned about a giant people. Then Israel should remember that God has defeated giants before, for Moab and Ammon. What God did for those nations he has promised to do for Israel. So, Israel, do not fear! God can be trusted. He is powerful to keep his promises. He is more powerful than giants and he has demonstrated that in the past!

It is worth noticing in passing 2:14 and 15. The Lord had sworn that the Israelite adult generation which disobeyed at Kadesh would perish before entering the land of promise. Even that promise, God has kept. Verse 15 shows God actively working to fulfil that oath: "Indeed, the Lord's own hand was against them, to root them out from the camp, until all had perished." God is completely trustworthy, even to the point of carrying out the punishment he vowed against the earlier generation.

Israel's Victories (2:26–3:11)

These lessons are also learned in the accounts of Sihon and Og (2:26–3:11). Unlike the case with Edom, Moab and Ammon, Israel is to engage Sihon and Og in battle. God's hand is in this encounter through and through. Moses makes that plain. It is God who has "handed over to you King Sihon the Amorite of Heshbon, and his land" (2:24). It is God who "hardened (Sihon's) spirit and made his heart defiant in order to hand him over to you, as he has now done" (2:30). We might notice that a recollection of God's dealings with Pharaoh in Egypt is no doubt an encouraging recollection for Israel. Nonetheless Israel is no passive recipient. It is only by acting in faith and obedience that Israel will receive these promises. God gives, but Israel is to "take possession" (v. 31). This is Yahweh and Israel working together.

The conquest of Sihon was complete. "There was no citadel too high for us" (v. 36). Compare that with Israel's fear at Kadesh: "the cities are large and fortified up to heaven" (1:28). The reason for the triumph against Sihon was not Israel's strength. Rather, it was God's. "The Lord our God gave everything to us" (2:36). The same applies to Og. The towns of Bashan "were fortress towns with high walls, double gates and bars" (3:5). Again, God's hand prevailed (3:3). Despite Og himself being a giant of a man, given by the size of his bed, a massive thirteen and a half feet long (3:11), he was defeated. God is all-powerful.

Moses is teaching that the fears at Kadesh about a tall and strong people with heavily fortified towns are not valid fears. Moses never downplays the strength of the opposition. Rather the strength of the opposition highlights the power of Yahweh. The conquests of Sihon and Og demonstrate that size, number and strength are no obstacle when Israel acts with faith and obedience. God is faithful. God is sovereign.

Of course the particular lesson from the Sihon and Og conquests is the huge encouragement they were for the remainder of the conquest. It is one thing to be taught that God is faithful and sovereign: these Israelites had seen this in action already. The forthcoming conquest on the other side of the Jordan merely extends what has already happened to Sihon and Og.

The details of the distribution of land taken from Sihon and Og follow in 3:12–17. This land is given to the tribes of Gad, Reuben and the half-tribe of Manasseh. The details and boundaries need not concern us here. The reason that Moses repeats these details is not to clarify what the boundaries are but to press home the point, with tangible evidence, that God is fulfilling his covenant promises. He promised descendants to Abram. We have seen that this promise by and large has now been fulfilled. He also promised land, a particular land and even that promise is now partially fulfilled. Two and a half tribes have already received their land, given by the Lord to occupy (3:18).

Step by step, Moses has demolished any reasons the Israelites may have had for being afraid and not trusting God in the forthcoming conquest of the land. He has shown them through recent examples, both positive and negative, that God is utterly dependable and able to achieve what he has promised. Through the repetition of the promises of God, which continues throughout Deuteronomy, Moses arouses and stimulates faithful obedience. There is no excuse for unbelief and disobedience. Like the faithful watchman later described to Ezekiel (see Ezek 33:1–9), Moses discharges his commission faithfully and thoroughly.

Moses' Own Failure (3:23–29)

Yet chapter 3 concludes with Moses' acknowledgement of his sin and his coming death. He will not enter the land (vv. 25–27). He has already referred to this in 1:37. Even Moses, the great leader and hero of faith, through whom God did extraordinary things, and to whom the Jews looked with great awe and respect, even he sinned and was to be punished.

It is sometimes argued that Moses' death is because of the sins of Israel and not for his own sins. This could be supported by the phrase "on your account" (1:37; 3:26). This would make Moses a suffering servant figure, not unlike Isaiah 52–53. However, Deuteronomy is also clear that Moses sinned (32:51). It is best to understand "on your account" as referring to the fact that Israel provoked Moses to sin.

The Bible is full of great heroes of faith. However, we must be very careful when learning from them. No one is perfect – except Jesus, the only moral example we can always follow. The same still applies. We should be careful not to view our Christian leaders or mentors today as perfect. When they sin we should be pained and sad, though perhaps not surprised, as all sin, even the great ones. Even the great heroes of faith need God's redeeming grace.

Moses reminds Israel that Joshua is to succeed him as leader of the people. That this is God's own appointment should encourage both Joshua and the people (v. 28). God is not deserting Israel or leaving the people on their own. The death of Moses hangs over the book of Deuteronomy. His failure to enter the land lends a sense of poignancy to the book, the imminence of his death adding urgency and passion.

God, the Giver of Land

Underlying much of the discussion about the land in Deuteronomy is the conviction that God gives land. The most common qualification Moses gives to the land in Deuteronomy is "which the Lord your God gives you" (1:8; etc.). Moses never tires of reminding Israel that God gives the land. He uses the word "give" as a rhetorical device to inspire renewed faith and zeal in the task ahead. This is the priority in Deuteronomy. God in his abundant grace gives the land to Israel. Yahweh's action of giving is fundamental and occurs prior to Israel's response. Yet the gift is only realized through Israel's own action of taking possession in faith and obedience.[2] This idea is developed later in Deuteronomy. The point to make here is that God is a gracious, freely giving God. This should hardly surprise us for it is made even plainer to the reader of the New Testament and God, after all, is one and the same.

It is also important to note that the promises on which the giving of the land depends are also promises of grace. The initiative is totally with God. The promises are unconditional. No conditions were placed on Abraham, nor are they placed on Israel. However, once in the covenant relationship, demands are laid. The demands indicate how to respond to grace, not the means by which God's favour may be won.

Throughout the Bible this is consistent. The Christian's relationship with God is initiated by God and freely established. However, the Christian is obliged to respond to such grace in faith and obedience. Deuteronomy is important for teaching God's people how to respond to abounding grace. Martin Luther described Deuteronomy as *"hoc libro maxime fides docetur,"* the book which teaches the most about faith, a very perceptive insight by the great reformer into the character of this book. It is a major theme to which we will return.

One of the issues Deuteronomy raises for Christians today concerns the land. We are familiar with the strife of modern-day Israel, the struggle for Palestinian self-rule, extremist Jews and Arabs who are opposed to peace and reconciliation, and the sharp contention over Jerusalem. It is easy to feel sympathy for both sides; for Jews so cruelly treated by Christians and Europeans in this century and earlier; for Palestinians uprooted from the land of their birth. We are probably familiar with various Christian points of view, which support one group or the other in the struggle for land. How should Christians, in the light of Deuteronomy, respond to such a question?

We need to remember that the possession of the land by the Israelites was initially in order for the blessing of other nations (see next chapter). Israel, through its subsequent history of failure, apostasy and idolatry in the land, forfeited its claim to possession. Hundreds of years after Moses, God sent

---

2. See for example, J. G. McConville, *Law and Theology in Deuteronomy* (JSOTSup 33; Sheffield: JSOT Press, 1984), 11.

Israel into exile. Though a number of prophets prophesied the restoration of the people of God in the Promised Land after the exile, for example Isaiah 40–66 and Jeremiah, the New Testament transforms those prophecies by focusing on the heavenly kingdom of God. The Christian, as the true descendant of Abraham, is promised an eternal, heavenly inheritance by God (1 Pet 1:4). No longer is geographical land a primary concern in the New Testament. Holy places give way to holy people, for the temple of God is now found in God's people, not a place.

This has important implications for how Christians respond to the warfare and destruction commanded in Deuteronomy. Since a geographical land is no longer promised to the people of God in the New Testament, there is no need for a physical or military conquest. The language of warfare taken up in the New Testament applies to the heavenly inheritance: whatever threatens the Christian's entering heaven is to be fought (Eph 6:10–18). Further, from the resurrection onwards, the people of God consist of Gentiles as well as Jews. There is no possibility for a repeat of any Old Testament holy war. Though part of Israel's conquest over the Canaanites was to inflict God's just punishment on sinners and idolaters, now the role of executor of God's judgment and justice is taken by Jesus Christ. It was accomplished in the cross, and not by the people of God as a whole (though in the preaching of the gospel, God's people function as agents of God's judgment to those who reject the gospel).

Sadly, passages like Deuteronomy (especially ch. 7) have been used to justify atrocities such as the Crusades. Then Christians viciously killed Muslims and others, in the name of God in order to reclaim Jerusalem and Palestine for Christendom. We must be careful to interpret Deuteronomy, and the issue of land, warfare and conquest in the light of the principles of the New Testament. Two things remain unchanged: God's holy judgment against those who reject him, worship other gods and practise idolatry, and the need for God's people to strive against anything and any temptation which will deprive them of realizing the promised inheritance of God. The call for holy living is as strong for Christians as it was for those who listened to Moses. In the Old Testament, the people of God were to express that holiness by separating geographically from people of other nations. In the New Testament, the people of God are to express that holiness while living scattered among people of every nation (1 Pet 2:12).

Trusting God

When Moses was called by God to lead Israel, he pleaded that he was slow of speech and slow of tongue (Exod 4:10). In Deuteronomy we see that he has become a great preacher for this book is his greatest sermon. For those who preach today, this is an important book. Moses aimed to stir up faith and obedience in the lives of his hearers, namely Israel. That is the concern of the New Testament too, whether in Jesus' command to "Repent and believe" (Mark 1:15), the sermons in Acts or Paul in Romans 1:5 where he uses the expression "the obedience of faith." It should be our concern too. Preachers can learn a lot from this book, from its theological principles, its means of building up faith and its rhetorical devices to exhort and persuade.

We have noted that grace is prominent in Moses' preaching and that he emphasizes the faithfulness of God to his promises. God keeps promises and is always working towards their fulfilment. He is powerful and able to do so. The promises to Abram were perhaps five hundred years old in Moses' day but they were still in force. Hundreds of years later, the birth of Jesus was because God was still keeping the promises made to Abram (see Luke 1:55, 73). Today God continues to bring about the fulfilment of those very same promises. Christians, who are children of Abraham through faith (Rom 4:16, 17), are, as promised, numerous. The Promised Land, though understood differently in the New Testament (Hebrews 4, for example), remains guaranteed to Christians. Another key promise to Abraham remains, that in him "all families of the earth will be blessed" (Gen 12:3). God is still, 4,000 years later, working to fulfil that promise too. Are you responding in faithful obedience to that promise of God? Can you see evidence of that promise being fulfilled?

The preacher today, then, like Moses long ago, needs to encourage faith in God's promises, assuring people that God has not abandoned what he has pledged. In today's world it is not easy to believe. Much around us seems to suggest God's absence, not presence, his faithlessness, not faithfulness. People need assurance that God is still faithful and still bringing about the fulfilment of promises made to Abram so many years ago. Throughout the centuries, God has not failed. Those promises apply to all God's people. They are worked out through Jesus Christ and, in particular, through his death and resurrection. The inheritance for the Christian, like the inheritance of the land of Canaan for the Israelites, is received through faith. Even more than the great and bountiful land of Canaan, the Christian's inheritance is greater still. For it is "imperishable, undefiled, and unfading, kept in heaven for you, who are being protected by the power of God through faith" (1 Pet 1:4, 5). What a great promise, and a great God, in which to have faith!

Questions for Discussion: Deuteronomy 1–3

1) Do we need sermons? Analyse the next few you hear (or preach). In what ways do they encourage or discourage faithful obedience?

2) Describe the character of God portrayed in Deuteronomy 1–3. How does this differ from and/or agree with what you know of God?

3) Step by step Moses has demolished all reasons for being afraid and not trusting God. What fears, attitudes or thinking are preventing you from trusting God's promises and obeying him? Can that be changed? If so, how?

4) These chapters are grounded in the faithfulness of God. How has God been faithful to you in the last month? week? day?

5) How can you better preach God's faithfulness to stir up obedience? Does preaching for obedience in your experience tend towards legalism?

Spend time in prayer, praying for a greater trust in the reliability and faithfulness of God. Pray that a remembrance of God's past faithfulness to you will stir you up in your service of him.

2

The God of the Covenant

Central to Deuteronomy is a lengthy exposition of many laws about how Israel was to live in the land (chs. 12–26). Before launching into this exposition, Moses needs to lay a foundation and framework for the right understanding of these laws in Israel's life. This he does in chapters 4 to 11. We will deal with these over the next two chapters. Deuteronomy 4 to 6 paints a clear picture of the nature of the relationship between God and his people. The laws, which are nonetheless important, are one aspect of this relationship.

The Privilege of Grace (4:1–40)

The initiative for a relationship with God lies with God. He acts first. Thus to be in a relationship with Almighty God is a huge privilege. This is the thrust of chapter 4. It is expressed in various ways. The notion of the faithfulness of God, so prominent in chapters 1 to 3, remains here also. Thus 4:1 refers again to the land as that which "the Lord, the God of your ancestors, is giving you." The faithful action of God in bringing Israel "out of the iron smelter, out of Egypt, to become a people of his very own possession, as you are now" is recalled in verse 20. The expression "his very own possession" is similar to what we read later in 7:6, "his treasured possession." The idea is of a special treasure, a prized possession, the thing which a person values more highly than anything else. Israel is treasured by Almighty God above anything else, an extraordinary statement, especially given its past failures. Relationship with this God is indeed an enormous privilege. No wonder the chapter praises God in rhetorical questions: "Has anything so great as this ever happened or has its like ever been heard of? Has any people ever heard the voice of a god speaking out of a fire, as you have heard, and lived?" (vv. 32, 33). What an honour to be God's special people. What a God, so worthy of praise!

God has initiated this relationship in love. "And because he loved your ancestors, he chose their descendants after them" (v. 37). Motivated by this love, God acted to redeem Israel from slavery in Egypt and to bring them into the land of promise (vv. 37, 38).

Given that this relationship is established by God, it must be evident that whatever the function of the law, it will not be to establish a relationship with God. Rather it can only be as a response to what God has done, and indeed, done in love.

The theological word which describes this disposition is grace. Though the word primarily occurs in the New Testament, the content of grace is apparent here too. It is helpful to think of grace in a threefold way.

- an attitude, here denoted by the word love expressing motivation (v. 37).
- an action in association with that attitude, here the signs of power in Egypt, the deliverance from Egypt, and the bringing safely to this point (vv. 34, 36–38).
- a gift, here the land being given (vv. 38, 40). The land is the grace place.

All three aspects function together. At its heart is generosity. The attitude is generous, for there was nothing about Israel to elicit love. The action is generous, for there was nothing about Israel to warrant redemption from Egypt. The gift is generous, for there was nothing about Israel to deserve the land.

This is the essential character of Almighty God. We shall see this expressed vividly throughout Deuteronomy. The New Testament abounds in statements about God's grace. "God so loved the world that he gave . . ." "The free gift of God is eternal life . . ." (John 3:16; Rom 6:23). As both of these statements in full show, Jesus Christ is grace personified. He is the greatest, most costly and most generous gift God could give, whose generous action in dying on the cross not only demonstrated God's extremely generous attitude to sinful people, but as Deuteronomy itself suggests, established us in a relationship with God himself (see for example Eph 2:8).

God's approach and character are consistent throughout the Bible. Sadly, we tend to misunderstand the Old Testament by thinking it to be law in contrast to the gospel of the New Testament and that the God of the Old Testament is a wrathful, merciless God in contrast to the merciful God of the New Testament. Deuteronomy 4 shows that not to be the case. Here we have a declaration that God is merciful (v. 31), meaning that God "will not forget the covenant with your ancestors that he swore to them" despite any future idolatry on Israel's part (vv. 28–31).

Yet it is also true that God "is a devouring fire, a jealous God" (v. 24). This is not some arbitrary or capricious anger. It is a desire for Israel's complete allegiance. He will tolerate no rivals in the form of idolatry. God wants a total response. He deserves nothing less. This jealousy is not a sinful attitude such as when we may be jealous of someone else's car or house or fortune. Rather it is like the jealousy of a husband for his wife or vice versa. Such a relationship properly expects an undivided loyalty. A husband's jealousy for his wife's faithfulness, and vice versa, are good things. God is like a marriage partner. He is jealous for his people's love.[1] Clearly then, the jealousy of God is actually part of his love for his people. It is a love that cares for the right response. That too we find in the New Testament. For example, Hebrews 12:29 calls God a consuming fire. The whole section, Hebrews 12:14–29, alludes to Deuteronomy 4. The grace of God in his revelation at Mt Sinai, which Deuteronomy 4 discusses, is exceeded by the grace of God's revelation in Jesus Christ. Increased grace and privilege does nothing to diminish the jealousy of God. Rather it heightens the affront which disloyalty causes.

Mt Horeb is important in Deuteronomy 4. At Horeb nearly forty years before, God spoke to all Israel giving them the Ten Commandments. He then gave further laws to Moses who at the time was on top of Horeb. God's presence at Horeb was demonstrated not only by the voice all Israel heard, but also by a fiery cloud on top of the mountain.

> You approached and stood at the foot of the mountain while the mountain was blazing up to the very heavens, shrouded in dark clouds. Then the Lord spoke to you out of the fire. You heard the sound of words but saw no form; there was only a voice. (vv. 11, 12)

What an amazing event. That Israel experienced such a theophany (the theological term for an appearance of God) was cause for some comment (see again v. 33). Generally, Israel expected that to experience God in such a close-up way resulted in death, as God was portrayed in terms like "devouring fire" (v. 24). Yet Israel had lived. This experience of God was an event of privilege and grace.

---

1. For the relationship between God and Israel expressed in marriage terms, see, for example, Hosea 2 and Jeremiah 3.

The Importance of the Law

This event also underscored the seriousness of the law. The heart of this theophany was what it revealed of God. God was not some mystical presence or mysterious voice. The purpose of his theophany was to reveal the will of God through the law. That the giving of the law was attended by fire and cloud underlined its importance. "You must not add anything to what I command you, nor take away anything from it, but keep the commandments of the Lord your God with which I am charging you" (v. 2). This law of God is not a "take it or leave it affair." It is his revealed will for how his people will live. It is the right and proper response to grace. The seriousness of the law is further shown by the reference in verses 3 and 4 to Israel's sin at Peor. There, those who sinned perished. See Numbers 25 for the account of this episode. This God of grace takes the law seriously.

In fact, as a prelude to expounding the laws from chapter 12 on, Moses wants the people to be in no doubt how important it is to obey. He urges obedience that requires great care and attention. "So now, Israel, give heed . . ." (v. 1). "You must observe them diligently" (v. 6). "But take care and watch yourselves closely . . ." (v. 9). "And the Lord charged me at that time to teach you statutes and ordinances for you to observe in the land" (v. 14). "So be careful not to forget the covenant that the Lord your God made with you" (v. 23). Moses himself had sinned and was being punished for it (vv. 21, 22). Any future sin of Israel would also be punished (vv. 25–28). The law is important. Care is needed to keep it. Obedience does not come naturally.

The law is itself a gift of grace, for the goal of the law is life, "that you may live to enter and occupy the land" (v. 1). This is shown graphically in verse 4: those who obeyed at Peor lived; those who disobeyed perished (v. 3). Verse 40, which ends this section, says similarly, "Keep his statutes and commandments, which I am commanding you today for your own well-being and that of your descendants after you, so that you may long remain in the land." Indirectly then, the law is a gift of life, the means to life. Thus we can understand why St Paul could say, "the law is holy, and the commandment is holy and just and good" (Rom 7:12).

This life which is held out and promised is not mere physical existence. In Deuteronomy life is always life "in the land," that is in God's place, and life lived under God's care and rule. Life is quality relationship to God, full of blessings because of that relationship. True life, life to the full, always has God at its centre. That is the life which Deuteronomy anticipates. It is the same sort of life Jesus came to bring (e.g. John 10:10; 14:6; 17:3).

The final point about the law here is that it reveals God's purpose beyond the people of Israel. "You must observe them diligently, for this will show your wisdom and discernment to the peoples, who, when they hear all these statutes, will say, 'Surely this great nation is a wise and discerning people!'" (v. 6). Since the creation, God has been concerned for all humanity. His election of the descendants of Abraham was not a rejection of the rest of the world. Rather God was working through the descendants of Abraham to restore all humanity to himself.

The obedience of Israel to the law would demonstrate the character of God to the world and would attract the world to God. That is, the law is evangelistic. This is an extraordinary concept. In some societies Christians have been caricatured as living dull lives deprived of pleasure because of the prohibitive commandments of a stern God. They mock Christian obedience and morality as being outdated, puritanical and prudish. In response to such pressure, Christians sometimes compromise, seduced into abandoning obedience to God to become "more relevant" and up-to-date for the world. This then leads to the other extreme where society sees no difference between Christian behaviour and the rest of society. Neither should be the case. Living as a faithful, obedient Christian is the best way of life there can be. It is the life of joyful and thankful response to a gracious God. It will be different from society's standards. Society will notice. Christians are never excused from obedience to God's law because we think it will distract others from God. If we fall into that trap we dishonour God and deserve to be called hypocrites. The best pleasure, the best life, is life lived in obedience to God. Upholding and keeping the unchanging standards of God ought never to be done begrudgingly but always joyfully. Though the world may from time to time mock the standards of God, there are always people searching for meaning and standards by which to live.

When the church compromises God's standards, rather than becoming "more relevant" to the world, it deprives the world of a means of being attracted to God. Most of us will know people whose initial attraction to the Christian faith and gospel was through the obedient living of Christian friends or neighbours. "They have something I don't have which I want," is their response. In effect they are paraphrazing Deuteronomy 4:6.

The reason that a right response to God's law has an impact is because the law fundamentally calls us to imitate God. God's own character and grace is evident in faithful and obedient Christians. We will see this more clearly when we look at some of the laws later. We were made in the image of God, yet it is an image marred by sin. The law aims to restore the image as the New Testament makes clear, though that restoration is only perfected through Jesus Christ, the one who perfectly lived the life of faithful obedience to the law (e.g. 2 Cor 3:12–18).

The Ten Commandments (5:1–21)

The most important part of the law was the Ten Commandments, sometimes called the Decalogue. Only the Ten Commandments were spoken audibly by God to all Israel and not just Moses, to whom God gave the rest of the law (see Exod 19:16–20:26). The Israelites had asked for Moses to mediate for them after receiving the Ten Commandments because of their fear at hearing the voice of God (Deut 5:22–27). Only the Ten Commandments were written by God himself on two tablets of stone which he gave to Moses to keep (see Exod 32–34). The reason for two tablets is best explained by ancient treaties which had two copies made, one for each party. These tablets were to be placed in the ark of the covenant, a place which symbolized the presence of God (Exod 40:20). It is no surprise then that Moses recites the Ten Commandments in Deuteronomy 5, at the head of all other laws. In addition there is a case to be made for the Ten Commandments being the guiding principle for the subsequent laws in Deuteronomy 12–26, or even 6–26. A number of scholars have attempted to show that the laws of these chapters follow the order of the Ten Commandments, beginning with laws about having no other gods except Yahweh. Not every law which follows fits into this pattern in an obvious way. Nonetheless it does suggest that what follows is a fleshing out of the Ten Commandments in more detail, showing a selection of applications of the general principles of the Decalogue.

To ensure there is no doubt that these commandments are binding on this current generation, Moses says, "The Lord our God made a covenant with us at Horeb. Not with our ancestors did the Lord make this covenant, but with us, who are all of us here alive today" (vv. 2, 3). Of course the previous generation had died out in the wilderness and those to whom Moses now speaks were either children at the time of the exodus or were born in the wilderness. Yet he wants to make it plain that this covenant endures and is as binding on these Israelites as on their parents. Deuteronomy will stress again and again the importance of teaching the faith to each generation, for the covenant is an abiding relationship with every generation of God's people. See below on the fifth commandment about honouring parents.

The commandments are immediately preceded by a statement about God. "I am the Lord your God, who brought you out of the land of Egypt, out of the house of slavery" (v. 6). These commandments are grounded in an already established relationship, indeed a relationship based on redemption, that is rescue from Egypt. This, then, is the response to that gracious redemption in a nutshell. So the law only has sense and meaning within a relationship with God established by grace. For those outside such a relationship, the law is meaningless and not binding. This issue is an important one for Christians concerned about the morality of society and behaviour of others. We are not justified in imposing the Christian law on others without bringing them into a relationship with God. The law on its own is incomplete.

While we must be careful not to artificially divide our responsibility to God and that to our neighbour into two separate things, nonetheless it is worth noting here that the first four commandments deal primarily with our relationship with God and the second six primarily with our relationship to other people. It must be remembered that the last six commandments are also about responding properly to God.

> You shall not make for yourself an idol, whether in the form of anything that is in heaven above, or that is on the earth beneath, or that is in the water under the earth. You shall not bow down to them or worship them; for I the Lord your God am a jealous god, punishing children for the iniquity of parents, to the third and fourth generation of those who reject me, but showing steadfast love to the thousandth generation of those who love me and keep my commandments. (Deut 5:8–10)

In the context of the imminent entry into the Promised Land, the commands to have no other gods and not make idols are critical. The land was full of other gods, gods of the polytheistic Canaanites (the Canaanites worshipped many gods), and there would be every temptation to follow such gods. Those gods were easy to deal with, undemanding morally and indulgent sexually. It was common in those days to think of gods as having control or dominion over a particular location. These Canaanite gods were gods of Canaan. Yahweh, the God of Israel, was an outsider and intruder. The pressure would be on Israel to change allegiance. God's word to this is a clear and blunt, "No."

No other gods, because I am the god who brought you out of Egypt. No other gods because I am the only other (4:39). Any other so-called gods are man-made creations. Your allegiance belongs to me and me alone. The command not to build idols (vv. 8–10) is based on similar reasoning. Whether the idols are attempts to represent God himself (as possibly 4:15–19 suggests), or are idols representing other gods, ultimately does not matter. Since God himself cannot be represented physically, as chapter 4 made clear, any attempt to do so really means the creation of another god.

The command against the worship of other gods and idols is amazingly frequent in Deuteronomy. If sins can be ranked, this is the worst and most serious sin. The issue of exclusive loyalty to Yahweh, and the rejection of Canaanite gods and practices, underlies many of the subsequent laws. It is the reason for the strict laws about the correct place of worship in chapter 12, the severity of punishment for false prophets in chapter 13, the food laws in chapter 14, and so on. Deuteronomy is very particular about keeping clear of Canaanite practices.

We must realize what a threat this was for the people of Israel. It would not be easy for them to resist. While as Christians we might not be able to imagine bowing down before a lump of wood or metal, the path to idolatry is a cunning and deceptive one. For idolatry is the end of a road begun with unbelief and disobedience. Where the road of unbelief and disobedience veers only gradually away from the straight road of faithful obedience, it is not always easy to tell the right road. That is why Deuteronomy so often urges Israel to "take heed" and "be very careful." Nonetheless as soon as we have moved even slightly off the straight road, our sense of direction is distorted and very quickly we are well off course, and careering towards outright idolatry. We must be careful. Like a car with faulty steering, humans veer off course. Without constant attention, we will all too soon be worshipping other gods and idols.

The danger is as great today, for the idols and other gods we face are possibly more subtle. They are not made of molten metal. Many of today's idols are good things in and of themselves, for example, security, family, good health and happiness. When we fail to trust God for these things, and keep God first in the process, we have set up idols for ourselves.

Verse 9 poses some difficulties. It seems that God is threatening to punish three or four generations of children for the sins of their idolatrous parents or grandparents. Is this really what God is like? A number of comments need to be made.

- Verse 10 balances the threat of verse 9 by showing that God extends his steadfast love to the thousandth generation. Thus God's steadfast love, a word which includes notions of mercy and grace, far outweighs his jealousy and punishment.
- It is true that later generations do suffer the consequences of the sins of their forebears, though the verse addresses the issue of punishment and not the consequences of sin.
- In other places in the Old Testament, it is specifically stated that children do not suffer unfairly for the sins of their parents. See for example Ezekiel 18.
- The verse is probably referring to children who continue the idolatry of their parents. That is, the children are not innocent. Deuteronomy has a strong emphasis on parents teaching their children the faith (see below on Deut 6:20–25). One of the consequences of idolatry is that the next generation is prone to continue in idolatry. There are many examples of this in Israel's later history. However, the children will not be able to say it is their parents' fault. They are responsible for their own sins.

> You shall not make wrongful use of the name of the Lord your God, for the Lord will not acquit anyone who misuses his name. (5:11)

The third command is not just about swearing. It was common in the ancient world to take binding oaths. To take an oath or make a promise in God's name, and not keep it, is to take his name in vain. Given what we saw in the previous chapter about God's utter faithfulness to his promises, we can understand why not keeping vows and oaths made in God's name means we take it in vain. God is a promise-keeping God.

> Observe the Sabbath day and keep it holy, as the Lord your God commanded you. Six days you shall labour and do all your work. But the seventh day is a Sabbath to the Lord your God; you shall not do any work – you, or your son or your daughter, or your male or female slave, or your ox or your donkey, or any of your livestock, or the resident alien in your towns, so that your male and female slave may rest as well as you. Remember that you were a slave in the land of Egypt, and the Lord your God brought you out from there with a mighty hand and an outstretched

arm; therefore the Lord your God commanded you to keep the
Sabbath day. (5:12–15)

The Sabbath command in Deuteronomy is grounded in the rescue from
Egypt (vv. 12–15). In Exodus 20:11, the same command is grounded in the
creation rest of God. Whatever the origins of the two different motivations,
the two fit together. The creation rest of the initial Sabbath day was recognition
of the perfection of the life God had made. The rest derived from redemption
from Egypt is to show the difference between being enslaved in hard labour
under an oppressive regime and serving Yahweh, "in whose service is perfect
freedom." The Sabbath day was to be a taste of the perfect life with God, a
foretaste of heaven, as Hebrews 4:1–11 suggests. It is not about mere physical
rest but rather the rest, or restoration, which alone comes from God. It is
to be a God-centred day, for in God alone comes real refreshment and life.
How wise God is. He knows our needs better than we do. How foolish we
are. So readily we rely on our own strength, ignore his provision and then
struggle stubbornly.

While the focus of the Ten Commandments now shifts to relationships
with others, God is not far from the scene. How we treat others is a reflection
of how we treat God. The laws in Deuteronomy make that very clear. The
person who covets (v. 21) expresses a lack of trust in God's generosity. The
person who steals (v. 19) does the same, and so on. At the heart of all these
laws is a right relationship with and appreciation of God. We will never be able
to keep these commandments if we haven't got a right relationship with God.

> Honour your father and your mother, as the Lord your God
> commanded you, so that your days may be long and that it may
> go well with you in the land that the Lord your God is giving
> you. (5:16)

Family life is very important in Deuteronomy. The fifth commandment to
honour parents underlines that. What this commandment is about is keeping
the faith of your parents, for Deuteronomy comes from the perspective that the
adults it addresses are followers of God. When that is the case, the children are
expected to keep this faith. The commandment obviously extends to general
care and respect as well but its key is the issue of faith. Children honour their
parents by keeping their faith in Yahweh. This is suggested by the motivation
at the end of verse 16: "so that your days may be long and that it may go well
with you in the land." That motivation occurs elsewhere in Deuteronomy and
its fulfilment depends on keeping faith in Yahweh. If children are going to be

able to keep this faith, the parents have the responsibility to teach it. While modelling and lifestyle are crucial, teaching is also necessary (e.g. Deut 6:7, 20–25). If you are a parent, you have an obligation to teach the faith. This is a reminder that Christian parents have a crucial responsibility in passing on the faith to their children. Likewise, we can never rest secure in the faith of our parents. We need to have and express our own faith.

> You shall not murder. Neither shall you commit adultery. Neither shall you steal. Neither shall you bear false witness against your neighbour. Neither shall you covet your neighbour's wife. Neither shall you covet your neighbour's house, or field, or male or female slave, or ox, or donkey, or anything that belongs to your neighbour. (5:17–21)

The next commandments prohibit murder (though this does not mean all human killing since Deuteronomy elsewhere commands the killing of Canaanites and also decrees capital punishment for certain offences), stealing and adultery. The Bible as a whole considers sexual morality and marital fidelity to be very important. Marital fidelity is a reflection of God's own love for us and how we ought to respond in faithfulness to him (e.g. Hosea; Eph 5:22–33). The ninth commandment has a legal setting. Bearing false witness will cause someone to be wrongly sentenced in court.

The final commandment, against coveting, balances the preceding five. It recognizes that sin stems from the heart of a person. Sin is not merely an external action somehow detached from the person. Evil actions stem from within, as Jesus' words in Matthew 12:33–35 show. We shall see that idea again in Deuteronomy.

Ten commandments were all the Israelites could take! They pleaded with Moses to act as a mediator for them, recognizing the holy greatness of God and being afraid in his presence. That this is the right response is seen in God's words, "If only they had such a mind as this, to fear me and to keep all my commandments always" (v. 29). Fear is an appropriate reaction to the presence of God for sinful people. Consider Isaiah 6:1–7. A sinner in the presence of Almighty God is in a dangerous position. That is why the writer to the Hebrews is so excited about the work of Jesus enabling us to come right up to the throne of grace (see Heb 4:16; 10:19–22). God seems to recognize here that it will not always be so. The problem, as addressed here, is the heart, just as we saw with the commandment not to covet.

Before we turn to Deuteronomy 6 it is worthwhile pondering briefly what place the Ten Commandments should have for Christians today. Views on this range from rejection to binding obligation and there is a great amount of literature on this topic. Why should we keep these laws but not, say, those about boiling a kid in its mother's milk? (Deut 14:21). This law is repeated three times in all in the Old Testament so it must have been of some importance. The Old Testament needs to be read through the eyes of the New Testament. Where the New Testament reinforces an Old Testament commandment, there is no dispute that Christians remain under obligation to that commandment. Likewise where the New Testament explicitly rejects an Old Testament law, Christians no longer are obligated to that law. The grey area is where the New Testament is silent on a particular law. With respect to the Ten Commandments, nine are reinforced explicitly in the New Testament. Indeed, in the Sermon on the Mount, Jesus strengthens some of the commandments, making it clear, for example, that murder includes hatred and adultery lust (Matt 5:17–37). The only one of the Ten Commandments which is not explicitly reinforced in the New Testament is the Sabbath commandment, though references to it occur in the context of a number of Jesus' miracles. Jesus' attitude to the Sabbath day ought to be a model for Christians. He restored people to health arguing that the Sabbath was made for people and not vice versa. That Jesus is the Lord of the Sabbath also indicates something about the character of the day (Mark 2:23–29). The practice of the early church in celebrating the day of resurrection suggests that the question of which particular day is not so important.[2]

Hear, O Israel (6:1–9)

Deuteronomy 6 continues with an even tighter summary of the required response of the people of God. This is what Jews call the Shema, the first Hebrew word of verse 4.

> Hear, O Israel: The Lord is our God, the Lord alone. You shall love the Lord your God with all your heart, and with all your soul, and with all your might. (6:4, 5)

Here in a nutshell is how God's people are to respond to God. Elsewhere in Deuteronomy, as we have already seen, is the expression "with all your heart

---

2. For further discussion, see D. A. Carson, *From Sabbath to Lord's Day* (Grand Rapids: Zondervan, 1982).

and with all your soul." Only here is "might" added, to highlight the great importance of this commandment.

Love is such a misunderstood word and concept. It is not primarily an emotion, at least as it appears here, but is a deliberate response to a command, regardless of emotion. Love is an act, an act of the will. Thus we decide whether we will love or not. We don't wait for some agreeable emotion to move us. What sort of act is involved? Exactly what we have read in the Ten Commandments: no other gods, no idols, honour of parents, respect of human life, and so on. We love on God's terms, not ours. We don't decide what seems a loving act; God does. How can we tell whether or not we love God? By testing our obedience. Such is also the message of Jesus (for example in John 15:10. Compare also the message of 1 John). To love God is to obey him, thankful for his grace in redeeming us. We love God because he first loved us (1 John 4:19).

This law governs all the other laws. When we read later laws in Deuteronomy, we misunderstand them if we fail to see that they can only ever be properly fulfilled from a heart loving God. This chief law guards against legalism, keeping the letter but not the spirit of the law. That is never possible. The response God wants is not external observation but total and unreserved obedience. What goes on in our hearts, inside us, and in the secrets of our minds is crucial before God.

The exact meaning of verse 4 is debated because the Hebrew has no verb. Most Bibles give alternatives in the footnotes.[3] The context nonetheless makes it clear what this verse means. It is a call to total and absolute allegiance to God. No other gods are to be contemplated. God will not tolerate two-timers. Even more, this verse is acknowledging that "our God" is Yahweh, the name revealed to Moses in Exodus 3. It is a personal name. It is a privilege to call God so personally. It is the name that stands for the relationship between God and his people. It is the typical way God is referred to in Deuteronomy. The name Yahweh, then, especially with the added "our God," is a clear reminder to Israel that they are dealing with a God who has made promises and redeemed them. This is not a remote God, as we saw in chapter 4, but a God of revelation.

---

3. The main options are: "The Lord our God is one Lord"; "The Lord our God, the Lord is one"; "The Lord is our God, the Lord is one"; "The Lord is our God, the Lord alone." Literally the verse reads, "The Lord our God, the Lord one." The key distinction is whether the verse is saying that Israel must have only one God or whether God himself is one or unique.

The importance of this for the people of God is underlined in the verses which follow. The centrality of the Shema for Jews today derives from here. Israel is to speak these words all the time, teaching them to their children, binding them on their hands and foreheads and writing them on their gates and doorposts (vv. 7–9). That Moses does not mean this to be taken literally can be seen from verse 6: "Keep these words that I am commanding you today in your heart." That is the governing statement. The following illustrates pictorially what the implications are. Wherever Israel goes (v. 7), whatever time of day (v. 7), whatever Israel does or thinks (v. 8), whether at home or away (v. 9), the command to love God applies, totally and unreservedly. Taking this literally misses the point. Our response flows from within.

Marc Chagall has a painting called "The Rabbi." The rabbi is fleeing, clutching tightly a Torah scroll with the words of the Shema showing. That is all he carries, his most treasured possession. That is how important the command to love God is. Our relationship to God is to be the most precious thing in our life, our treasure, our joy, our most valuable possession, not worth risking or losing at any cost. Jesus said much the same. "The kingdom of heaven is like treasure hidden in a field, which someone found and hid; then in his joy he goes and sells all that he has and buys that field" (Matt 13:44).

The Promise of Paradise (6:10–25)

Then follows one of the two breathtaking highpoints of grace in Deuteronomy. Verses 10–15 describe the land that Israel is to inherit. It was promised on oath to the patriarchs, a guarantee of future possession (v. 10). Yet, what a land! Fine large cities, houses full of goods, cisterns already dug out, and vineyards and olive groves ready for fruit. It all sounds like a holiday brochure! This is grace abounding for God does not give any land but gives a great land. All the work is done. When we remember that the supply of water in a land like Israel was always critical, we realize how great this promise is. Huge amounts of effort were needed to dig wells and underground cisterns, cut into rock, to preserve safe water. Today visitors to the Holy Land can still see the massive cisterns at Masada, the wells at Arad and the tunnels in Jerusalem which show how wonderful was the promise of ready-made cisterns. It is ready for living. Its abundance is indicated by the end of verse 11, "and when you have eaten your fill . . ." We can imagine the five star hotel!

What an incentive for Israel to claim the promise of the land. This is paradise revisited, the place of perfection. The toil promised to Adam after his sin in the garden of Eden is no longer. Yet a warning is attached. Satisfaction is dangerous for faith; prosperity is a faith hazard; plenty brings complacence and forgetfulness. "Take care that you do not forget the Lord" (v. 12). When we think we have made it and have all we need, when everything is readily supplied and on tap, it is easy to forget God, the supplier of all we have. The warning is timely today. Prosperity attacks faith. In Western society, most of us don't consciously regard God as provider, for regardless of whether there is seasonal rain and sun or not, the supermarket shelves have all we want. Robust Christian faith is under attack in modern, wealthy society. We need to heed this warning, "take care that you do not forget the Lord."

The proper and positive alternative follows, as always. Never is there only a warning about what not to do; there is always some corresponding, appropriate, positive action to take. "The Lord your God you shall fear; him you shall serve, and by his name alone shall you swear" (v. 13). Again there is a warning against following after other gods, balanced by another exhortation to keep God's commandments (vv. 14–19). Moses' model is a good one for Christian preachers who do well not only to warn against wrong behaviour, but in its place commend appropriate and positive conduct.

Finally in this chapter, in the context of teaching children, the law is again set in its rightful place. "What is the meaning of the decrees and the statutes and the ordinances that the Lord our God has commanded you?" (v. 20). The law is not primarily a policeman. It is not the path to God nor the means of getting right with him. But, as the answer to this child's question shows, the law is the thankful response to the grace of redemption (vv. 21–23). Indeed it is argued that in these verses, the giving of the law is part of God's redemption, being a mark of ownership of the new master, God, who bought a slave from some other master, in this case Egypt. Thus the law is an indication of an existing relationship and faithful obedience to the law is the right expression of a relationship to a redeeming and holy God.

Here we return to where Deuteronomy 4 began. The law is "for our lasting good, so as to keep us alive, as is now the case" (v. 24). God knows what is good for us. Keeping the law is wisdom (4:6) for the law is righteous and just (4:8; hence 6:25). All too often we want to decide what is good for us. We think that modern, sophisticated and liberated people can add or take away to improve or update God's law. However, we don't know best. Only God does. That is why we are told not to alter God's word (4:2). When we try to run things our way, even as well and fairly and lovingly as possible, it falls far short of God's best way. He has shown us what is good. We don't need to look for it; he's told us. Our task is to do it – for our good.

Questions for Discussion: Deuteronomy 4–6

1) In Deuteronomy 4, God is described as both jealous and merciful (vv. 24, 31). What do you understand by this description?

2) The first commandment was that Israel was to have no other gods but the Lord (5:7). Similarly, 6:4–5 says that Israel was to love God alone. In your country, in what ways do Christians *not* put God first? How have you addressed that in your preaching?

3) Ancient Israel was to be separate from other nations, in part to remain uncontaminated by the idolatry of those nations and in part to be a role model for the world (4:5–8). How should Christians be in the world and yet different from it?

4) Does the Sabbath command have implications for Christians today?

5) How can we keep God's words in our hearts today? (6:6) How does this verse make us think about the importance of preaching?

Spend time in prayer, praying for a greater holiness in your life and a stronger resistance to conforming to this world while living in it. Read Romans 12:1, 2.

3

The God of Discipline and Grace

When we are sick, we pray to get well. When we are in need, we pray for that need to be met. When we are grieving we pray for comfort. When in distress, we pray for relief. It is good to pray. Yet should these be our first prayers? For those who do pray, we often turn too quickly to request an end of the situation which will bring restoration. We claim that God wants health, joy and relief. We find Bible verses to support that. We say that God loves us and therefore he will quickly right the wrongs. There is nothing wrong with this but ultimately such thinking has too narrow a view of God's love. For God is concerned more about us as people, who we really are, than he is about our situations. Our situations, whether good or ill, poor or rich, or whatever, are means, not ends, to God's overwhelming love for us as people.

God uses the situations in which we find ourselves to develop us into the people he wants us to be. Our first prayers should not be for ease but for education, not for health but for growth. We should be asking God to show us what we are meant to learn and how we are meant to grow as Christians. We will never get this right if we have a this-worldly focus and goal. If that is the case, we desire fulfilment in this life and look forward to a time now when all is right and good. When we have an eternal perspective we realize that all things will only be right in the life to come and, more than that, that we too need radical change. The most important change that needs to be made is in us, not about us. This does not mean we should never pray for relief, for the psalms teach us how to do that. It is our priorities that matter.

To add another dimension to this, if we are slow to learn from the troubled times we are even slower to learn from the good. Subconsciously we have a "works-righteousness" mentality, that is, we think that when our situation is going well, we are OK before God. That need not be the case at all. When our situation is good, we are still, if not more so, in need of learning and growing.

The Discipline of Love (8:1–6)

Deuteronomy 8 is profound. It balances the issues so simply. The Israelites could easily have thought that their time of testing was over and now, in the land, things would be fine. After all, the land has already been described in such glowing terms (e.g. 6:3, 10, 11). Yet the point will be made clearly that both in bad times as well as good the Israelites need to be careful to learn. This chapter has a strong and deep understanding of the love of God. His love is strong enough to discipline us, as a father does his children. This is not wimpy, watery love but robust, rigorous love. This is love that really cares.

Israel's time of forty years in the wilderness was due to its sin at Kadesh. Apart from Caleb and Joshua, the entire Israelite adult generation that left Egypt would die in the wilderness and it would be their children who would take the land. This period was not simply a time of punishment, like being locked up in prison until the time for release arrives. It was a correctional time, a time of discipline and learning. Moses made that clear in verse 2: "Remember the long way the Lord your God has led you these forty years in the wilderness, in order to humble you, testing you to know what was in your heart, whether or not you would keep his commandments." Yes, it had been tough. Yes, it had been long. Yes, the people had found it difficult. The reason was that God was not punishing them so much as training them. God takes no delight in punishing but his love is so extensive that he uses our failures to train for good.

God was concerned to humble Israel for, as Deuteronomy 9 explains, Israel was proud and self-reliant. The strange events of the wilderness period may puzzle us. Water out of a rock? Manna from heaven that does not come on the Sabbath day? Were such strange things God's showmanship? Was he aiming to impress with dazzling displays of magic? See Exodus 16 and 17 for the account of this. No, the strangeness of this provision was to make it undeniable that the provision came from God. There was no other answer. If God had provided "normally," his hand as the supplier would be less obvious. All attempts to try and explain rationally the manna from heaven as sap from a tamarisk tree or some other substance fail to account for the double supply that came every Friday morning with none on Saturday. The only possible answer is God!

This is what Moses is referring to as testing and humbling. The circumstances arranged by God led to one conclusion – God, and one response – trust. So Moses says in the next verse: "He humbled you by letting you hunger, then by feeding you with manna, with which neither you nor your ancestors were acquainted . . ." (v. 3). The hunger was humbling. The feeding was humbling. So not only the need but also the provision was disciplinary. The aim? It was "in order to make you understand that one does not live by bread alone, but by every word that comes from the mouth of the Lord" (v. 3). God was drawing the Israelites to total and utter trust and dependence on him, training them to trust his reliable word, training them for obedience in the land of promise. As we saw back in Deuteronomy 4, life is not mere physical survival but rather life with God. Hence it depends on God and what he gives, every word that comes from his mouth. Note that this verse is not saying that spiritual things are more important than physical things, as commonly thought. The verse affirms we still do live on bread. However it draws Israel to appreciate the source of life, God. It is God who provides bread. It is also God who provides life.

This was not a harsh, punitive God at work. Rather this was the hand of a loving father. "Know then in your heart that as a parent disciplines a child so the Lord your God disciplines you" (v. 5). This is real love at work, the love of a good parent. It is not the New Testament alone which recognizes God as a father. The relationship is rooted in the Old Testament. Because our society has such a weak understanding of love it fails to see the loving discipline of God. He is still the same, allowing his creatures freedom to act but all the time lovingly and eagerly seeking to discipline them to love and trust and obey his word. "Now, discipline always seems painful rather than pleasant at the time, but later it yields the peaceful fruit of righteousness to those who have been trained by it" (Heb 12:11).

This wilderness testing is important also for the light it sheds on Jesus. It was no coincidence that in his own temptation (or trial or testing) in the wilderness Jesus' three statements to the devil came from Deuteronomy 6 and 8 (e.g. Luke 4:1–13. Jesus quotes from Deut 8:3; 6:13 and 6:16). Jesus is not just "proof texting." He is making a striking claim about himself. His forty days clearly correspond to the forty years of Israel. His temptation is preceded by a statement of his relationship to God – that he is the Son with whom the Father is well pleased (Luke 3:22). Now comes the demonstration of true sonship. Where Israel failed, Jesus succeeded. Where Israel yielded to temptation and didn't learn from the discipline, Jesus faithfully trusted God. Jesus is what Israel should have been. That they were not, is why he came. Through him alone, through his perfect obedience alone, can we also come to be adopted sons of the Father (1 John 3:1).

The lesson then is clear: "Therefore keep the commandments of the Lord your God, by walking in his ways and by fearing him" (v. 6). This applies in any situation, for the focus now shifts to the future life in the land. As already suggested, while the land itself is superb and has nothing wrong with it, the concern is how the people will live in it. This is the issue for the rest of the chapter. If Israel has learned its lesson in the wilderness, then it ought to be able to reapply that lesson to a new, entirely different situation.

Applying the Lessons (8:7–20)

Verses 7 to 10 again describe this land. Again the land is said to be superb, a clear contrast to the wilderness time. "Flowing streams, with springs and underground waters welling up in valleys and hills" (v. 7) contrast with the wadis of the wilderness which only flow some of the year. In the land, there is a reliable water supply. "A land of wheat and barley, of vines and fig trees and pomegranates, a land of olive trees and honey" (v. 8) contrasts with the lack of variety and abundance in the wilderness. "A land where you may eat bread without scarcity" (v. 9) yet again is a stunning promise to people who have only known wilderness living. "You will lack nothing, a land whose stones are iron and from whose hills you may mine copper. You shall eat your fill" (vv. 9, 10) complete the picture.

Those who have travelled to Israel may ponder at such a description. Today Israel and Palestine seem so bare, desolate and rugged, we wonder why anyone would fight for the place. However we ought to remember that it has not always been thus. Apparently the climate of Palestine hundreds of years ago was much wetter than today. There has also been an enormous deforestation over the centuries, in part through wars and also through taxation of trees during the Ottoman empire. Both led to a disastrous destruction of trees with consequent erosion, loss of fertile soil and change of rainfall.

After forty years in the wilderness Israel has almost made it. The people have been tested by God; disciplined by their heavenly father. Now, surely, they have made it? No, for a further time of testing and discipline awaits them. The goodness and abundance of the land is also a test, a time of discipline. It is not the harshness of the wilderness by any means but a different sort of test. "Take care" – sometimes translated "be very careful" – "that you do not forget the Lord your God" (v. 11). How can Israel forget God? This is not simply a memory test, as if the Israelites must remember God's name. The test of remembrance is clear: "by failing to keep his commandments"

(v. 11). Disobedience is forgetfulness. Lack of faith is forgetfulness. A good memory is very important for a person of God, not a memory for names and places and dates, nor even a memory of Bible verses or an ability to recite them. Remembering God results in obedience and faith. We may be able to memorize the whole Bible yet, if disobedient and unbelieving, we are actually forgetful.

Memory is still important for Christians. This can be seen from Jesus' words at the Last Supper the night before he died. "Do this in remembrance of me" (Luke 22:19). Jesus is not wanting ritual remembrance. He wants obedient faith. The Lord's Supper is a means God uses to stimulate that obedience and faith. The real test is in the living. How well do we remember Jesus during the week, Monday to Saturday?

Prosperity is a strong temptation and we require great discipline to respond to it properly. This is the warning in the remaining verses of chapter 8. Houses, herds, flocks, silver, gold, in fact everything, will be multiplied (vv. 12, 13). What then? The danger is pride. Israel could so easily think: "My power and the might of my own hand have gotten me this wealth" (v. 17). Such self-exaltation is forgetfulness of God (v. 14). The lesson from the wilderness has been that everything comes from God. There it was patently obvious that God was providing. That is what Moses reminds them in verses 14 to16. God does not stop providing when there is plenty and provision seems effortless. God is still the supplier.

What an important lesson today. For all the talk of "mother nature" and the earth giving life, God is forgotten. Sadly today "back to nature" is not back to God and "concern for life" is not necessarily concern for God. We have supermarkets open twenty-four hours a day because we just might want to buy crushed pineapple from the other side of the world at 4 a.m., or we run out of breakfast cereal at 11 p.m. We complain if our shops run out of eggs or if there is a bakery strike. How easy it is to ignore the fact that God is the provider. It is not always easy to say grace at meals with sincerity because we take our food for granted. Yet we must heed the warnings, avoid forgetting, and "bless the Lord your God for the good land that he has given you" (v. 10). It is interesting to note that rural communities are usually more religious than urban dwellers. One reason for this may be that those in the country more obviously depend on God for rain and sunshine in their seasons. Those who live in the city take these all for granted, complaining one day when it is too hot and another when it rains. City dwellers tend not to see as clearly that a divine hand is behind the weather.

God's gifts – his generous grace – are freely given, but they have as their goal our training, or disciplining, for our good. We began this chapter by saying that God is supremely concerned about us as people, even more than about our situations. He wants us to be like him, and like his son who alone resisted all temptation. "For the grace of God has appeared, bringing salvation to all, training us to renounce impiety and worldly passions, and in the present age to live lives that are self-controlled, upright and godly" (Titus 2:11). The Israelites have experienced and seen the grace of God as well. Their delivery from Egypt, preservation and guidance in the wilderness, and the giving of a bountiful land (vv. 14–16) was the grace of God, grace given for training to live godly lives.

The chapter finishes with another warning against idolatry. This is where forgetfulness will lead. The gods of the Canaanites were fertility gods whose tasks were to provide produce from the land. This was the danger of the land of Canaan. Moses has made it clear that fertility of the land is Yahweh's work, not the work of the so-called gods of the Canaanites. Forgetting God results in his being replaced by other idols or gods. The implication is that this is folly. God, Yahweh, is the sovereign provider. The worship of anything else is the worship of the provision, not the provider; the worship of the creation, not the creator. Idolatry is shortsighted and amnesiac. We need to see beyond the provision to the God who provides, keeping an attentive memory in faithful obedience.

Justified by Faith (9:1–6)

What follows in chapter 9 and into chapter 10 is one of the most astounding parts of the Old Testament. It has been described as the closest the Old Testament gets to St Paul. It repays careful attention.

Moses has already dealt with one trap of pride into which Israel may fall, the pride of wealth and abundance. A more basic trap is now dealt with at some length. If Israel does cross over the Jordan and conquer "nations larger and mightier than you, great cities fortified to the heavens, a strong and tall people, the offspring of the Anakim,"[1] what a great victory and national celebration there will be! What a time for national pride! When Australia defeated the mighty United States in the America's Cup in 1983, a nation larger, more powerful and wealthier than it, national pride went sky high as

---

1. See our discussion on the Anakim and giants of the land in chapter 1.

the nation exuberantly celebrated and boasted. One can hardly imagine Israel doing anything else in similar circumstances.

Yet the trap is subtle. Israel would do well to see and acknowledge that God, Yahweh, had fought and acted for them. The conquest is not really their work. The deeper question is why God should do so. The answer Israel could easily arrive at would be: "It is because of my righteousness that the Lord has brought me in to occupy this land" (v. 4). After all, back in Genesis 15:16, God had said the land would be given to Israel as punishment for the sins of the nations which inhabit the land. The conclusion, surely, was that Israel was more righteous.

Not quite. Yes, the nations are wicked: "It is rather because of the wickedness of these nations that the Lord is dispossessing them before you" (v. 4). Yet, and here is the key, "It is not because of your righteousness or the uprightness of your heart that you are going in to occupy their land" (v. 5). Why then is God acting? God is acting to punish, certainly. He is also acting to keep his covenant promises made to Abraham, Isaac and Jacob (v. 5). As we have seen already, God is faithful.

Surely, though, there must be something righteous about Israel to warrant this? Wrong. God, through Moses, repeats the statement about Israel's righteousness not being motivation for God's action (v. 6). Up to this point the question of Israel's righteousness has been left ambiguous. It could be concluded thus far that while this righteousness was not the motivation for God, Israel was, nonetheless, righteous. That conclusion is demolished by a little addition to the repeated statement at the end of verse 6 – "for you are a stubborn people." Extraordinary! It is all very well for God to punish wicked nations but why give their land to a stubborn people?

The answer is, in effect, none other than what St Paul calls "justification by faith" (e.g. Rom 3:21–31; Eph 2:1–10). This theology is not restricted to the New Testament. Here it is in Deuteronomy 9. To be "justified" is, simply, to be accepted and forgiven by God, declared by him to be righteous. The motivation for this is God's love, which we have already called grace. "It was because the Lord loved you and kept the oath that he swore to your ancestors, that the Lord has brought you out with a mighty hand, and redeemed you from the house of slavery, from the hand of Pharaoh king of Egypt" (7:8). Israel is no better than the other nations. Yet it is being given this land because of Yahweh's immense and gracious love. That is grace, an undeserved, unmerited love. "Love to the loveless shown, that they might lovely be."[2] Not love to the lovely, love to the worthy or love to the righteous, but love to the unlovely, the stubborn, the unworthy. That is grace.

It is important to realize that the heart of justification is the atoning death of Jesus on the cross. There he took the sins of God's people, enabling God to justly declare his people righteous. That is the argument of Paul in Romans 3. That then is why Deuteronomy 9 does not in fact deny the righteousness of Israel. Through grace Israel is righteous, just like Christians are today. For righteousness before God does not mean sinlessness in this life. Rather, our sins are dealt with through Jesus' death. For the Israelites, the same applies even though they lived before Jesus. Through faith their sins also were atoned on the cross of Christ.

This is the second highpoint of grace in Deuteronomy. The first peak was the picture of the absolute generosity of God's grace seen in the unsurpassed splendour of the land like the garden of Eden (6:10–11). Now we see so clearly the unworthiness of the recipients. Israel stands before God about to receive an abundantly good land, with everything it needs. Yet, as chapter 9 will go on to show, and 1:19–46 has already shown, Israel was completely undeserving of God's love. It had repeatedly and consistently failed God. It had no claim on the land at all. Yet God is gracious, generous and loving. We stand before God in a similar position, unworthy of our salvation and any of God's good gifts. We didn't deserve Christ to die for us. Yet God's grace extends all the way to us, to sinful people, motivated solely by God's love and faithfulness to his promises. We have no grounds for pride, every reason for praise.

A Rebellious People (9:7–24)

Deuteronomy 9 continues to outline the reasons why God can call Israel stubborn. There are so many that Moses can say: "you have been rebellious against the Lord from the day you came out of the land of Egypt until you came to this place" (v. 7). What a damning indictment of a people so spectacularly rescued. Yet, sadly, it is true. It didn't take Israel very long to start complaining. In fact they hadn't even got to the Red Sea! (see Exod 14:10–12). Time and time again they complained and yet God did not give up on them.

The low point in this sad tale occurred at the very point where there should have been a good response, "even at Horeb" (v. 8). At the very time

---

2. "My Song is Love Unknown," Samuel Crossman.

Moses was on Horeb receiving the Ten Commandments and the rest of the covenant laws, when God had come down to his people in fire and thunder and cloud, and when the Israelites had heard the actual voice of God, they sinned. Such an experience doesn't take long to rub off! If anything, the timing of Israel's sin shows how strong sin is, how much it has mastered even the privileged people of God. Seeing a miracle or theophany of God doesn't deal with our sin. It may be a spur to faith for a short time, but that time may be very short indeed. That is why our faith does not depend on such experiences and miracles. We must be careful not to rely on experiences of God, but to be thankful for them when they occur.

Israel's sin was to make an idol, a golden calf, to worship, and Aaron was induced to take a key role in making it. The whole event is first narrated in Exodus 32-34. Its repetition in detail here shows what an important lesson needed to be learned from this past failure. Moses was on Mt Horeb with God receiving the two tablets of stone inscribed with the Ten Commandments (vv. 9-11). God knows what is happening below and tells Moses that he has seen their idolatry (vv. 12-13). "Let me alone that I may destroy them and blot out their name from under heaven" (v. 14). This is no idle threat. If we think God is manipulating Moses' response with a threat he has no intention of carrying out, then we misunderstand the character of God's holiness. This is serious stuff!

Moses goes down the mountain and, seeing the idolatry, smashes the two stone tablets (vv. 15-17). The covenant is broken by Israel's sin, the smashed tablets signifying the end of the relationship with God. It is over. Moses fasts and prays (vv. 18-20) and then destroys the idol (v. 21). This was not the only occasion where Israel had failed and been stubborn against God. Moses lists a few of the other occasions (vv. 22, 23). For Taberah, complaining at hardship, see Numbers 11:1-13; for Massah, complaining at the lack of water, see Exodus 17:1-7; for Kibroth Hattaavah, complaining at the manna from heaven, see Numbers 11:7-35. Kadesh has already been discussed in Deuteronomy 1:19-46 (see also Num 13 and 14). The summary is devastating: "You have been rebellious against the Lord as long as he has known you" (v. 24). Any claim Israel may have had for righteousness is now washed completely away. The people of God, who personally had experienced liberation and redemption from Egypt, who had seen first hand the provisions and guidance of God, are through and through a stubborn people. Yet, despite such rebellion, they will still receive the land, as the beginning of Deuteronomy 9 says.

Why didn't God keep his word to destroy Israel? Did he really change his mind? Was there something in Israel after all that made him keep on with them? Just in case there remains any lingering doubt, Moses tells Israel what he prayed. This is an important prayer for it shows one effective instance of prayer prayed according to the will of God. No excuse for Israel is given. No mitigating circumstances are adduced. No blame is passed. Full responsibility is accepted for the sin. That is the first point to notice. It is acknowledged that sin is sin and the threatened punishment is fair. In New Testament times also, "the wages of sin is death" (Rom 6:23). We are flirting with danger when we try and excuse our sin and fudge repentance. Confession of sin requires acceptance of responsibility and acknowledgement of its seriousness in God's sight. Most of us find this hard work. We hate to admit our mistakes and our pride leads us to blame parents, education, neighbours, family, dog, boss, weather or the government. If we do not "take the can" for our own wrongdoing before God, we will never confess our sins as we ought.

Praying for Mercy (9:25–29)

> Lord God, do not destroy the people who are your very own possession, whom you redeemed in your greatness, whom you brought out of Egypt with a mighty hand. Remember your servants, Abraham, Isaac, and Jacob; pay no attention to the stubbornness of this people, their wickedness and their sin, otherwise the land from which you have brought us might say, 'Because the Lord was not able to bring them into the land that he promised them, and because he hated them, he has brought them out to let them die in the wilderness.' For they are the people of your very own possession, whom you brought out by your great power and by your outstretched arm. (9:26–29)

Moses' prayer is based on three points. First, he appeals to the fact that God has redeemed these people (v. 26). These "people are your very own possession, whom you redeemed in your greatness." Moses is saying, "don't let your work of redemption be in vain." Indeed God and Moses pass responsibility for the people back and forth to each other. In verse 12, God calls the people "your people, whom you have brought from Egypt." He passes them to Moses. In turn, Moses reminds God that they are his own people. He passes them back to God. Note the repeated second person pronouns in verse 26. Moses is emphatic: they are your people, God, not mine!

Second, Moses appeals to God's promise to the patriarchs (v. 27), namely Abraham, Isaac and Jacob. If God destroys Israel, he is breaking his promise. In fact, in verse 14, God had said he would make Moses the father of a new people. The temptation for Moses to accept this offer must have been great. To start again with Moses seems to suggest breaking the promise made initially to Abraham, though Moses is a descendant of Abraham. Moses, to his credit, resists temptation and keeps God to his word. "Remember your servants, Abraham, Isaac and Jacob." These three patriarchs are frequently mentioned in Deuteronomy. We noted them in 1:8. Almost always, their mention is to underscore the promise of land to Israel. The allusion continues here. Remember them, God, by giving the land you promised to their descendants. Moses knows God is supposed to be faithful and in this prayer he is calling God to account for his faithfulness to his promises.

Third, Moses appeals to what the other nations would think (v. 28). Why should that matter? Because the honour of God's name is at stake. If God destroys Israel, other nations will think God is weak and to be mocked. Moses is ultimately concerned for the honour of God's name.

There is a lot to learn from this prayer. Moses balances justice and mercy. He acknowledges what is right, yet he prays for mercy, based on the promises of God, the acts of God and the honour of God. If we want to pray like this, we need to know the promises of God carefully and ask God to keep them. We should remember that God has acted to save us in Jesus and so we need to pray that Jesus' death is not in vain. We should also note that there is nothing selfish in this prayer. Its concern is for God and the honour of his name. This should be a motivation for us in our praying.

Why should we pray for strong churches? Or for church unity? Or for effective evangelism? Or for people to become Christians? Or for forgiveness for Christians who have sinned? Ultimately we should pray for these things because they honour God. We may want strong and growing churches in part because they encourage us, boost our sense of achievement in ministry, excite us, and so on. Yet even more important is it to realize that when the church is weak and divided, when Christians sin and fail, God's name is not honoured in our society. It is humbling to realize that God stakes his reputation on our character and behaviour. When we fail or are weak, God is dishonoured. Christians have an awesome privilege and responsibility in carrying the reputation of God himself. It makes our failure all the more serious. A few years ago, the bishop of the diocese where I was ministering resigned after admitting a gross sexual indecency. The public ridicule of the church was extremely sad. But even worse, the dishonouring of God's name was blasphemous. We ought to pray boldly like Moses, who prayed in the face of God's anger and threats, and who stood in the breach, all for the sake of God's holy name.

Answered Prayer (10:1–11)

This extraordinary prayer was answered. God changed his mind. Though we find it hard to rationalize this, in the end we need to accept the fact that prayer accomplishes things. We do not have to be a great hero of faith to pray effectively. Though Moses was a hero of faith, and so too Elijah, James makes the point that Elijah was a human being just like us (5:17). He could as easily have used Moses as his example. For the person of faith, prayer is effective. So pray, and pray boldly.

Chapter 10 begins with the command to Moses to prepare two more stones for the Ten Commandments (v. 1). The covenant remains. The relationship is restored. Note how these verses stress "like the former ones," "the same words as before." This is to underline the point of restoration of relationship. It is interesting that the word "tablets" occurs seven times in 10:1–5, the same number as in 9:9–17, suggesting that the second pair is a complete replacement for the first. The relationship is fully restored. Second, the bracketed section, verses 6 to 9, shows that while Aaron did eventually die, the priesthood, which he represented, continued through his son and through the Levites. In 9:20 Moses prayed for Aaron, singling him out from the people because he was the leader of their sin. Thus 10:6–9 shows that this part of Moses' prayer is also answered. Finally, 10:10, 11 describe the command of God to continue the journey. Israel's sin is graciously forgiven. The repetition of basic covenant commands in 10:12–22 shows that the covenant relationship begun at Horeb is reinstated after the sin of the golden calf.

It is important to remember that despite the answer to prayer, despite the extension of mercy and renewal of the covenant relationship, Israel remained unchanged. There is no hint anywhere in the account of the golden calf, nor in Moses' prayer, that Israel is now changed or different. Moses does not appeal to God saying Israel will do better next time or they won't do it again. The implication of the narrative is that Israel is probably just as likely to repeat its sin. Indeed, this next generation, despite the testing and trials and discipline, is still, as the present tense underlines, "a stubborn people" (9:6). They are as guilty as their fathers. Change is not a prerequisite for mercy or salvation; that would be salvation by works.

It is also worth noting in passing that while God has forgiven, he obviously hasn't forgotten. The common misconception that to forgive is to forget is dangerous. If we have been hurt deeply by another, we may never be able to forget. We can still forgive. To forgive is to treat as if the sin did not occur, to act towards the sinner without bearing any attitude affected by that sin. That is what God does with Israel.

To sum up, Deuteronomy 9:1–10:11 takes away any possible grounds for the people of God to think that God's amazing acts are motivated by their worth or value. The Israelites are no better than anyone else. They are sinners needing mercy. In this light we realize how astonishingly good God really is. We can offer him nothing at all to contribute to or warrant his attention and salvation. Yet, because of his boundless love, he considers us worth saving through the death of Jesus. We can never finish plumbing the depths of divine love.

Yet as we have constantly seen, this love calls for a response. We can hardly receive such a great gift without being changed in our relationship to the giver. Christian ethics, how we live and behave in relationship to God and in this world, is well described as an "ethic of thankfulness." For God wants our willing, heartfelt obedience and faith. He does not want a grudging, reluctant legalistic obedience. Considering the riches of his grace, that is not at all unreasonable. As we have already seen, he wants us to love him with all our heart and soul and strength. We shall see in some of the laws which follow that God commands generosity on the part of his people in response to his own generosity.

The section which immediately follows, 10:12–22, the content of which is dealt with in the study at the end of this chapter, sums up all of Deuteronomy so far. We must never separate our response from God's prior action. Only when we keep these two firmly and properly linked will we respond to God as we ought.

Questions for Discussion: Deuteronomy 10:12–22

Deuteronomy 10:12 begins "So now…", that is, in light of this long description of Israel's stubbornness. What follows, then, is a summary of what God expects of his people, a prescription for avoiding stubbornness.

1) What does it mean to fear the Lord? (This expression occurs many times in Deuteronomy. An answer to this question also considers the parallels to fear, namely, here in Deuteronomy 10, walk, love, serve and keep.) How do you motivate your people to fear, love and obey God when you preach?

2) "The Lord set his heart in love on your ancestors alone and chose you" (v. 15). Why did God do this? In what ways can you say that God has chosen you? Do many Christians in your country simply call themselves Christian because of their ancestry? How can you stir them up to make a personal commitment to God?

3) What is the relationship of verses 18 and 19? How would you describe the character of what is demanded of God's people in the light of verse 19?

4) In many ways, these eleven verses summarize Deuteronomy. In your own words, write a brief summary of the message of Deuteronomy for Christian people. What do you see are the similarities and differences for Christians compared to the original Israelites?

Spend time in prayer, praying for a more complete and total devotion to the service of God.

4

Worshipping God

In this chapter we shall concentrate on the major laws relating to the worship of God. In the same way that the Ten Commandments began with laws relating directly to God, so the laws of Deuteronomy 12–26 begin with laws about how to worship God. In our next chapter we shall look at some of the laws concerning relationships within the Israelite society.

God Has Spoken (12:1–7)

In our modern, secular society the importance and priority of laws about directly worshipping God can hardly be overestimated. The trap of humanism is the lie that our love of and duty to our fellow human being is the sum total of appropriate worship of God. Christians will not want to downplay our love of neighbour yet even before this the Bible tells us to love and worship God in right and proper ways. While from one angle the direct worship of and relationship with God may look impractical or cut off from the so-called real world, we are reminded again and again in Deuteronomy (and indeed all the Bible) that private and public worship and service of God is to be central to any real life.

Undergirding all these laws lies a fundamental, theological principle. God has revealed himself. God has spoken. The only way we can know how to appropriately worship God is that he has told us. We are not to worship God in our own ways or "according to our own desires" (12:8) because God has told us how to worship him in the Bible.

This is not to argue for rigid uniformity of Christian worship everywhere, though we always need to conform to the principles of scripture. The importance of this theological principle today is that it is becoming popular to think of God as a large mystery, a "cloud of unknowing." Christian worship then becomes an exercise in approaching a mystical, mysterious God and will lack certainty or assurance. While we can never claim to know everything about God, nonetheless, God has revealed all we need to know – in his Son and in the Bible. He has detailed the essentials of how we are to worship him and what it means. Fundamentally then, it is not a mystery but an act of obedience to a revealed God.

Exclusive Worship

Another most important area this principle addresses, both today and, as we shall soon see, in Deuteronomy, is the false idea that since there is one God, any worship is worship of that God. "We all worship the same god anyway," we are told. Such statements ignore completely Deuteronomy 12, let alone most of the rest of the Bible which consistently regards the gods of other nations as idols and not the true, living God of the Bible. The context of these laws in Deuteronomy is that of the worship of other gods by the inhabitants of the land. It was a pluralist world as ours is today. Yet the worship of their so-called gods is clearly not worship of Yahweh. It is expressly forbidden. "You shall not worship Yahweh your God in such ways" (12:4). Why not? Because Yahweh has revealed himself and worship as the Canaanites practised it ignores the character, purposes and acts of Yahweh. Such ignorant worship is very rude, to say the least.

This principle is extraordinarily important as seen by the vigour of the following:

> You must demolish completely all the places where the nations whom you are about to dispossess served their gods, on the mountain heights, on the hills and under every leafy tree. Break down their altars, smash their pillars, burn their sacred poles with fire, and hew down the idols of their gods, and thus blot out their name from their places. (12:2–3)

There is not much room for tolerance here! The words stress the total and absolute obliteration of these practices. Why? There are six reasons.

- The gods of the Canaanites were false gods and not Yahweh. Since Israel belonged to Yahweh by virtue of his choice of Israel and redemption of it from Egypt, allegiance to any other god was detestable.

- Worship of these gods was prohibited because these gods had not acted to redeem Israel. As we shall see later, a key part of Israel's worship was the remembrance and thanksgiving for redemption.
- Worship of these gods was wrong because Yahweh was the God of all, including the land they were about to enter. He was not a territorial god restricted to the wilderness at all. The land was his.
- Worship of the Canaanite gods was wrong because Yahweh was the God who provided everything – rain, sun, produce. This has been stressed in the early chapters of Deuteronomy (e.g. 8:7–10, 12–18).
- Worship of the Canaanite gods was prohibited because it was immoral, involving cultic prostitution and child sacrifice as means of trying to win the favour of the gods to give fertility (12:31).
- Such worship was prohibited in these strident terms because with its slack demands and immorality it was a temptation to Israel. There is always a seductive appeal in other gods which demand little and promise much. Israel was to strenuously resist such temptation. If Yahweh is the only God, there is no place at all for any worship of other supposed gods.

I have listed these reasons because it is important to see that behind the positive commands for proper worship is not a desire for Israel to be different for the sake of being different. The difference derives from Yahweh, who is immensely different from the gods created by the imaginations of the Canaanites.

Verse 5 begins the positive commands. "But you shall seek the place that the Lord your God will choose out of all your tribes as his habitation to put his name there. You shall go there . . . ." This "place" contrasts with the "places" of Canaanite worship in verse 3. This is worship on Yahweh's terms, not Israel's. It is to be at his place.

This command for so-called "centralization of worship" has been one of the key issues for scholarship on Deuteronomy in recent decades. It is argued that only one place is in mind, namely Jerusalem, which was where, under King David up to four hundred years later, Israel's capital was established and, under Solomon his son, the temple was built. Deuteronomy never mentions Jerusalem by name. Nor is there any clear indication that a building like a temple is envisaged. The point of the verse is that worship of Yahweh is not to occur where the worship of Canaanite gods occurs. The place is Yahweh's choice, not Israel's, and not Canaan's. The Canaanites worshipped their gods on the top of hills and under green trees, places which suggested closeness to the sky and fertility. They were perhaps natural places to construct shrines. Israel was to avoid all contact with those places.

Whether verse 5 (and similar expressions elsewhere, e.g. vv. 11, 14, 18, 21, 26) implies one unique place or more than one place is debated. Certainly sacrifices and worship are expected at Mt Gerizim in Deuteronomy 27, but Israel's history shows central worship in Shiloh, Bethel, and other places before the temple in Jerusalem was built. The command for central worship makes a lot of sense at the beginning of Israel's history. Sociologically it would be an important unifying factor for the twelve tribes. The ark of the covenant, containing the Ten Commandments, was a symbol of God's presence with his people. Though the ark is not often mentioned in Deuteronomy, it is significant in the books of Samuel and 1 Kings. There was only ever one ark and the place where it resided would logically become the current place of central worship. Indeed, when the temple was built, the ark was placed in the Holy of Holies within the temple. Thus the temple in one sense continued the function of the ark which had been in existence as long as Israel was in the land.

The Presence of God

Wherever the place described in chapter 12 was, and Deuteronomy deliberately does not mention any names, in some special way God's presence was there. Thus the offering of sacrifices and eating was "in the presence of the Lord" (12:7, etc.). This is probably what is meant by the statement in verse 5 that Yahweh would "put his name there." His name implies himself, his presence, though some scholars have argued for a distinction between the dwelling of God's name and his presence.

The presence of God is a critical biblical theme. The Bible begins with humanity in God's presence, but the sin of Adam and Eve results in their expulsion from this presence. Thereafter the Bible story is about how humanity can come again into the presence of God. So the Bible shows a progressive approach by God. There are occasional theophanies and visions to the patriarchs (Abraham, Isaac and Jacob) and Moses, and then symbolically cloud and fire through the wilderness represent a more constant presence. The ark of the covenant stabilizes this presence in the land. It is later incorporated into the temple as a solid, reliable and, supposedly, permanent statement of the presence of God. The detailed liturgical rules of approach into the temple show the importance of this theme. Ultimately the temple is destroyed, and the exile begins, due to Israel's repeated sin. Yet in Immanuel, "God with us," Jesus is a living temple, a closer approach than stones and altars were.

Two final stages complete the progress. The Holy Spirit dwelling within Christians is God's intimate presence with his people. Finally, in the New Jerusalem, the holy city of heaven, there is no temple because the dwelling of God is with humanity (Rev 21:3). Thus the statement about a central place is a statement of grace. The almighty and holy God graciously chooses to dwell with his people, not as closely as in Eden, yet not insignificantly either. It is a down payment for his closer presence to come. Worship then is relational, for God is neither remote nor unknown, but close and near and known (Deut 4:7). That is a great encouragement. The Israelites have been promised God's help in conquering the land (e.g. 7:19). That presence will be a permanent feature of the land. It is on the way to a recreated Eden, as we noticed in a previous chapter. This central place, the place of Yahweh's choice, is the focus for all the laws related to corporate worship in the next few chapters.

For Christians, tracing this theme throughout the Bible shows that our worship is not geographically restricted to a particular place but personally restricted to a particular person. Jesus is the focus for Christian worship, not Jerusalem nor any other place. God's presence with his people now is different and closer than in Old Testament times.[1]

Sacrifice and Joy

The central place in Deuteronomy is the focus for sacrifices and offerings. "You shall go there bringing there your burnt offerings and your sacrifices, your tithes and your donations, your votive gifts, your freewill offerings, and the firstlings of your herds and flocks" (12:5, 6). The complete regulations and specifications for sacrifices are given in Leviticus 1–7. Moses does not repeat those here. They are already known. Not all sacrifices are mentioned here though all the different types of sacrifices are understood by the general "burnt offerings and your sacrifices." Sacrifices had various functions. Not all dealt with sin. Some were for thanksgiving, others for fellowship. Interestingly, the most important annual sacrifice, the Day of Atonement sacrifice is not mentioned at all in Deuteronomy. Possibly this is because Deuteronomy wants to paint an idyllic picture of life in the land and motivate the Israelites

---

1. Jesus' discussion with the woman at the well turns on this point. See John 4:20–24. Also see Matthew 18:20; and Stephen's speech in Acts 7.

by positive ideas. The Day of Atonement focuses on the need for atonement because of sin.

The idyllic picture is captured in verse 7. "And you shall eat there in the presence of the Lord your God, you and your households together, rejoicing in all the undertakings in which the Lord your God has blessed you" (12:7). This verse raises two more points which recur in other laws regarding worship. First, there is a specific inclusion of households. This is spelled out in verse 12: "with your sons and your daughters, your male and female slaves, and the Levites who reside in your towns" (similarly 12:18; 14:26, 27). In addition, for the third year tithe in 14:29, there is provision not only for Levites, but also the resident aliens, the orphans and the widows (similarly with laws about feasts, 16:11, 14). These statements reflect a key concern of Deuteronomy for the landless. The land is so important in this book – not least as the place of blessing – that those without land are singled out for special care. These are the servants, the Levites (who as the tribe of priests had no tribal territory, v. 12), the orphans and widows and the resident aliens (or sojourners, those who come from other lands but choose to live in Israel's land and accept its laws). Lack of land is to be no impediment to shared blessing. God's abundant provision will be enough for all.

The other point verse 7 raises is that of rejoicing. This law is a command to rejoice. Primarily rejoicing is not an emotion of joy, though that is important. Rejoicing is an act of the will, regardless of emotion. The emphasis on rejoicing is important motivationally. We all look forward eagerly to good times ahead, whether the sleepless child the week before Christmas or the tired worker anticipating a holiday. So the suggestion of rejoicing encourages the Israelites to obedience. Not only so, but also the idea of rejoicing is an acknowledgement of the faithfulness of Yahweh. It is a statement that the land will indeed be full of riches and blessing as previous chapters have promised. There will be enough for the landless to share. The abundance is for all.

This command to rejoice is a reminder that basic to all of life and its situations, the person who knows God can, and should, rejoice. Why? Because a relationship with God, as a person redeemed by his grace, is more enduring, more significant and more important than the day-to-day trials and concerns. Relationship with God vastly outweighs all the dilemmas and distresses of this world. Thus, for the Christian as for the Israelite, both redeemed through extraordinary grace, we can and should rejoice always. "Rejoice in the Lord always; again I will say, Rejoice" (Phil 4:4).

Indirectly then, this command is a call to get a proper perspective on things. Our sadnesses and sorrows, losses and lacks, are not trivial. Yet they are not the be all and end all of life. Unchanging and undiminishing is the grace of God in which we can always rejoice.

Deuteronomy 12 is, typically for Deuteronomy, an interweaving mesh of themes (or "leitmotifs") and key words. The repetition of motifs and words serves various functions. It underlines and stresses the importance of these ideas. There is a rhetorical, motivational function as well, for repetition can be a persuasive technique. Repetition also can suggest different nuances in different contexts. We must remember that there was a reason for repetition of ideas in such a motivational book as Deuteronomy and seek to appreciate it, rather than skipping over what seems repetitive.

Worship in the Land (12:8–27)

Though in verses 8 to 12 there appears to be much repetition of the preceding verses, there is a shift of focus. The context of verses 1 to 7 was the avoidance of Canaanite practices. Now the context becomes the change from current practices in the wilderness. The land is a different situation from the wilderness and therefore requires different practices. This focuses attention onto the character of the land. There is also the new idea of rest in verse 9 – looking forward to the completion of the conquest and the end of military action and threat. It is an anticipation of a settled life, with God as the focus. The rest also gives an additional reason for rejoicing. The Levites are now expressly mentioned in contrast to verse 7. While the repetition, then, stresses again the importance of this central place of worship, and the offering and rejoicing in God's presence, in the first paragraph the clear context was anti-Canaanite practices. Now it is in contrast to wilderness practices and, by looking forward explicitly to rest and settlement, is another added incentive to the people.

The next paragraph, verses 13 to 19, focuses on the provision for the slaughter of animals for eating in the towns and places where people lived. Not every killing was a sacrifice. God provided food as well. Killing for food was a different matter to ritual sacrifice and this is made clear here.

> Yet whenever you desire you may slaughter and eat meat within
> any of your towns, according to the blessing that the Lord your
> God has given you; the unclean and the clean may eat of it. (12:15)

Behind this allowance is the suggestion that the land will be plentiful. "Whenever you desire" suggests great freedom, as does "within any of your towns." No restrictions here. Even the unclean may eat. The unclean were the ritually unclean whose bodies or health had some illness or condition or deformity. In worship, perfection was expected, represented in the division of clean and unclean. When it came to general eating though, the distinction is done away with. Anyone can eat, anywhere, anytime. What a place this land will be.

The next paragraph, verses 20–27, elaborates on this theme in the context of enlarged territory. Will God's blessings ever end? This suggests another reason for slaughtering meat at home, namely the distance to the central place of worship. A long journey to a central place to slaughter one's dinner is not very user-friendly. God's laws provide for the people's good life in a good land. Their character is clearly not oppressive.

The Threat of Idolatry (12:28–13:18)

The chapter ends with a return to the context of anti-idolatry. A typical warning to "Be careful to obey all these words" is given (v. 28) signifying something very important. The motivation is "that it may go well with you and with your children after you forever" (v. 28). The acknowledgement that Canaanite worship will be a snare or temptation is stated in verse 30. Their worship is "abhorrent," a strong word denoting something fundamentally opposed to Yahweh.

This anti-idolatry context continues in chapter 13 which, while not specifically about corporate acts of worship, nonetheless fits the general theme of worship. The chapter divides into three cases of someone leading others astray into idolatrous worship.

- In verses 1 to 5, it is a false prophet or dreamer.
- In verses 6 to 11, it is even a relation or intimate friend.
- Verses 12 to 18 concern some scoundrels who actually succeed in leading a village astray.

The three cases build up momentum. The first is of a false prophet, someone who may be personally remote or not well known. The second case strengthens the force of the warning by identifying the potential deceiver as a close relative or most beloved friend. The stress is on the closeness or intimacy of the person. The threat may lie close at hand. Then the third case adds to the momentum for it describes a case where the deception has actually succeeded in leading a town astray. This makes it even clearer that the threat is indeed a strong and subtle one.

It is easy to be deceived. The false prophets actually speak words which do come true! How easy it is to believe such people. The test of them, then, is not whether what they say happens or whether what they try to do works. The test is to see where they are leading. God's people need to be careful for false prophets exist in any generation. The New Testament testifies to that also (e.g. Mark 13:22). We need to be careful and shrewd in testing their validity rightly. The threat of the close relative or loved one is also dangerous. It is easy to be misled by someone we love greatly because we don't carefully critique what is being said and imagine it unlikely such a person would mislead. The example of the town in the third case leaves no doubt that the threat is real. Thus, the effect of these three cases is to make it clear that the danger is real and extreme care is required. The right worship of and allegiance to Yahweh requires extreme caution.

Finally we should notice the punishment due to the offender, as well as to any led astray. There is little room for tolerance here. They shall be put to death (vv. 5, 9, 15). "Show them no pity or compassion and do not shield them" (v. 8). Why?

- What they have done is an extremely abhorrent act against God.
- The punishment is a deterrent for the people (v. 11).
- The character of sin is that it is powerful and spreads like a cancer. It needs to be cut off, destroyed from the root. Hence, "you shall purge the evil from your midst" (v. 5).[2]

Sin is a poisonous root which needs to be dealt with at its root, not its fruit or symptoms. That indeed is why Deuteronomy is so rhetorical, seeking to change, strengthen, and fix minds and hearts, the insides of people, the root of their being, to wholehearted and devoted worship of God. We ought never underestimate the power of sin to take hold of our life.

Tithes (14:22–29)

The next passage to look at is 14:22–29. This passage discusses the offering of tithes.

---

2. This a common refrain in the laws of Deuteronomy. Also, e.g. 17:12; 19:13, 19; 21:9, 21; 22:21, 22, 24.

> Set apart a tithe of all the yield of your seed that is brought in
> yearly from the field. In the presence of the Lord your God, in
> the place that he will choose as a dwelling for his name, you shall
> eat the tithe of your grain, your wine, and your oil, as well as the
> firstlings of your herd and flock, so that you may learn to fear the
> Lord your God always. (14:22–23)

Literally tithe means a tenth. Each year a tenth of all produce, animal and
cereal, is to be taken to the central place and offered. However the offering
becomes in effect a large party for it is to be eaten by the offerers (v. 23). The
mind boggles at such consumption! Again the whole household is included
as are the Levites (vv. 26, 27) and again rejoicing is commanded for the tithe
law presupposes the blessing of God. It anticipates the goodness and bounty
of the land. There will be plenty for all.

The consideration of God is illustrated by allowing produce to be changed
into money, which is readily transportable, to make travel to the chosen
place easier. God does not want to make unreasonably difficult burdens for
the people.

The purpose of this law is worth noting: "so that you may learn to fear
the Lord your God always" (v. 23). To fear the Lord is a relational act. It does
not mean being afraid of some unknown being but, rather, having a proper
and reverential relationship with the known God. Further, the notion of fear
overlaps in a sense what we call faith or trust.[3] This best explains the purpose
of the tithe law here. By giving a tenth each year as an offering to Yahweh,
the worshipper is expressing trust that Yahweh will continue to provide and
supply. One might expect the Israelite to store the surplus to cover lean years
or to use it to expand and grow. Alternatively, it may be that the Israelite
may want or need the tenth for the present. However, this law directs trust to
Yahweh, forcing the Israelite to consciously depend on, or fear, him.

The chapter concludes with an additional tithe every third year. This is
explicitly for the benefit of the landless. As the land is the site of blessing,
Deuteronomy is careful to ensure that the landless do not miss out.

---

3. Interestingly, the words for faith or trust are quite uncommon in Deuteronomy, though
see 1:32. Yet the idea underlies everything. The verb "fear" is very common (over thirty times
including derived forms, though not all to do directly with relationship to God).

Firstlings (15:19–23)

> Every firstling male born of your herd and flock you shall consecrate to the Lord your God; you shall not do work with your firstling ox nor shear the firstling of your flock. You shall eat it, you together with your household, in the presence of the Lord your God year by year at the place that the Lord will choose. (15:19–20)

Deuteronomy 15:19–23 contains the laws of offering firstlings, that is the first cattle or sheep. Two points need to be made here. Again the law is an expression of trust for it is the first that is offered, regardless of how many, if any, follow. To offer the first expresses trust in God that he will provide more. The second point this section makes is to emphasize that the best goes to God. "But if it has any defect – any serious defect, such as lameness or blindness – you shall not sacrifice it to the Lord your God" (v. 21). God deserves the best and the first. That is the priority.

This remains an important principle. The tithe is not the extra bit left over or the loose change at the end of the day. It is a tenth regardless of how much is produced. The law of firstlings shows the priority even more clearly. God's portion takes precedence. This is a challenge to Christians today to ensure that what they give God comes first. Too often we give God, whether time, money or attention, what is left over or spare. The principle of putting him first is crucial. If Christians give sacrificially enough to force a conscious dependence on God, our relationship with him will be greatly strengthened. The pressures of our society demand that we are secure – that we know where our next pay is coming from and our future is firm. God wants us to trust him, not our accountants.

Feasts (16:1–17)

The final verses to consider concerning the laws about corporate worship are those about the major feasts in 16:1–17. The Israelites had three major feasts which still today are celebrated by Jews. The Passover and Feast of Unleavened Bread is the first (vv. 1–8). This is to commemorate the exodus of Israel from Egypt (Exod 12:1–20). In our calendar, this feast occurs in March or April. In one sense it is a re-enactment. The food to be eaten included unleavened bread, for that was quicker to cook and on the original Passover night. Haste was important. A sacrifice is made, typically a lamb, though Deuteronomy actually permits an animal from the herd (v. 2). Possibly the Feast of Passover and Unleavened Bread had agricultural associations, as verse 9 indicates it is linked with the beginning of a harvest: "Begin to count the seven weeks from the time the sickle is first put to the standing grain." Probably this refers to the barley harvest.

The second feast was the Feast of Weeks, seven weeks after Passover (vv. 9–12). Its other name is Pentecost, from the Greek for fifty days, counting inclusively. No historical event is linked here to this feast, though verse 12 says, "Remember that you were a slave in Egypt." It seems to be largely an agricultural feast, probably at the time of wheat harvest. However, the Feast of Weeks came to be linked in Israelite history to the giving of the law at Mt Sinai since the period of seven weeks was about the time it took Israel from leaving Egypt to get to Mount Sinai.

The third feast is Tabernacles or Booths (vv. 13–15). Again this feast is linked to an agricultural harvest, probably grapes and olives. This feast falls in September or October. Little reason is given for this feast in Deuteronomy. That should not be of concern, for detailed instructions had already been given in Leviticus 23 for all the feasts. Remember, Deuteronomy is not giving details of the law but is rather urging obedience to the already-given law, knowledge of which is presupposed. The feast of Booths in particular commemorates the provisions of God throughout the wilderness years. The tabernacles or booths were tents made of branches and leaves to recall how Israel lived in the wilderness. It also recalled the leading of God through the wilderness by the cloud and fire and his provision of water from a rock and manna from heaven.

All three feasts were to be pilgrimage feasts. All the males, at least, were to go to the central place described in chapter 12, three times a year.[4] The three feasts were to be times of remembrance, which as we saw in a previous chapter, had the purpose of leading to obedience and faith. In this chapter the dominant note is, again, rejoicing. These are real parties, real celebrations. What God has done for Israel is to be a cause for lasting and deep joy.

It is useful to consider the place of these feasts for Christians. Is the instruction here to keep these feasts binding on Christians today? To answer that question, we need to see what happens to these feasts in the New Testament. Most of us will readily know that Jesus was crucified at Passover

---

4. Possibly the Passover was not always a pilgrimage feast but at times a family festival at home. See Exodus 12.

time. He was our Passover sacrifice, our Passover lamb (1 Cor 5:7). The New Testament makes much of the fact that Jesus' death is a new exodus, a release and redemption not from slavery in Egypt but, even more profoundly, from slavery to sin. This is indeed a greater exodus, for it deals with the hearts of people and not only with their external circumstances. If Israel was to celebrate so joyfully its redemption, how much more should Christians celebrate with joy! Christians then are called to celebrate Jesus' death as the focus of their redemption and salvation. Fundamentally this will be through the celebration of the Lord's Supper. The description of Jesus' last meal with his disciples in Matthew, Mark and Luke indicates that it took place in the context of a Passover meal.[5] Though our celebration of the Lord's Supper is not strictly a Passover meal, for Christians it takes the place of the Jewish Passover as a celebration.

The Feast of Weeks or Pentecost figures prominently, of course, in Acts 2. There the disciples, after Jesus' ascension to heaven, receive the gift of the Holy Spirit. The Old Testament law explains why so many people were in Jerusalem at this time for they were making their pilgrimage, even from foreign countries where, in Jesus' time, many Jews lived. Yet there is also a greater significance. The old feast of Pentecost recalled the giving of the law at Sinai. The new Pentecost sees the fulfilment of that with the giving of God's Spirit to "make you follow my statutes and be careful to observe my ordinances" (Ezek 36:26).[6] The law is now not written on two tablets of stone but written on the hearts of God's people by his Spirit. So Christians look to a greater law-giving than Mt Sinai, though we should also note that God's law is not done away with in the New Testament.

The third feast, Tabernacles, receives its major New Testament attention in John 7. Here, on the great day of the feast, Jesus said, "Let anyone who is thirsty come to me" (v. 37). As God provided water in the wilderness, this is "fulfilled" in a deeper way through the giving of the Holy Spirit, "rivers of living water" flowing out of the believer's heart (v. 38). As God provided in the past, now it is Jesus himself who provides endless water which provides real, spiritual life. Another aspect of this feast is alluded to in John 8:12 where, the next day, after all the candles in the temple had been extinguished, Jesus said,

---

5. In John's gospel, the emphasis is on Jesus' death occurring at the time of the Passover sacrifice, rather than the meal being a Passover meal. See John 13:1; 19:14; compare Mark 14:12ff. For a fuller discussion, see L. L. Morris, *John* (NICNT; Grand Rapids: Eerdmans, 1971), 774–786. Morris suggests that calendrical confusion may be the reason for the difference.

6. Jeremiah 31:31–34 has the same idea, though in different words.

"I am the light of the world." The candles signified God's guidance of Israel by a pillar of fire in the wilderness. Against such a backdrop, his statement is profound. As God had guided in the past, Jesus claims that role now. What an astonishing claim!

All that these feasts commemorated – the great redemption and provision of God – are fulfilled in a greater, deeper and permanent way by Jesus Christ and his death for us. This recognition should stimulate the Christian, even more than the ancient Israelite, never to forget what God in Christ has done, to rejoice deeply and celebrate salvation, to include others in this celebration and to give God all the honour, all the glory and all he is due, in lives of faithful obedience. His immense grace deserves far, far more than our leftover offerings. If the Israelites were to love God with all their heart, all their soul and all their strength, we have even more reason to do so.

Questions for Discussion: Deuteronomy 14

The context of the food laws is crucial for understanding their intention and meaning. The reasons for these laws are not so obvious to us today and we have to work a bit harder to find them out and then to know how to apply them to us today.

1) What are the issues relating to worship that your church faces?

2) What are the key issues of Deuteronomy 12 and 13? What is the key warning?

3) The immediate context of the food laws is spelled out in 14:1–2. Note that 14:2 is the same as 7:6. What warning did 7:6 follow? What is suggested, then, about the thrust of these laws in Deuteronomy 14?

4) Why does God make a threefold distinction in verse 21 between what Israel is allowed, what aliens can be given, and what foreigners could be sold? (Aliens were people from other lands who had chosen to live in Israel's land and adopt its ways.) In what other areas of life do Christians in your country need to show more distinctiveness from non-believers?

5) The command at the end of verse 21 about boiling a kid in its mother's milk came to be developed by strict Jews into a prohibition of cooking meat and milk products together. This is a basic kosher

cooking law. The reason was to ensure that there would be no accidental cooking of a kid in its mother's milk, for you could never be sure otherwise. Is this response a fair one in the light of the principles behind these laws?

6) How would you respond today if someone offered you pork, or perhaps, jelly blood to eat? What New Testament principles come to bear on these laws for Christians?

Spend time in prayer asking for God's help in discerning today's idolatrous practices and for wisdom how to preach in such situations. Give thanks for the freedom Christians have through Jesus.

5

Loving Your Neighbour

Love of our neighbour is part of loving God. In Deuteronomy this is made clear in many ways. The summary of the law in 6:4, 5, which refers to the love of God with all the heart, soul and strength, is a summary of all of Deuteronomy's law. Even where the laws do not specifically speak of an attitude to God but only deal with human relationships, we understand that such relationships reflect our relationship to God. Second, in some of the laws dealing specifically with worship practices, Israel is explicitly commanded to care for the landless, namely the widows, orphans, sojourners or aliens, and Levites. Humanitarian concern is properly an expression of worship to and relationship with God. That is the context, then, of this chapter.

In this chapter it is possible only to discuss a few of the laws in Deuteronomy 12–26. We shall highlight some of the principles of these laws and give some suggestions for their application for current times.

Attitudes (15:7–11)

The laws in Deuteronomy deal as much with attitude and intention as with external action. This is illustrated in 15:7–8:

> If there is among you anyone in need, a member of your community in any of your towns within the land that the Lord your God is giving you, do not be hard-hearted or tight-fisted toward your needy neighbour. You should rather open your hand, willingly lending enough to meet the need, whatever it may be.

This is hardly a law that can be dealt with in a court, for how could a court judge a person's intentions or attitudes? Yet, even though a human court may be unable to prosecute under such a law, God knows the hearts of human beings and that is what he searches out (e.g. Ps 139). It is obviously up to each person to carefully work out what is generous and what is not in this case. What is generous for one person may well not be so for another, as Jesus' parable about the widow's mite taught (Mark 12:41–44). Christian obedience is not only a matter of doing the right thing, but doing it for the right motivations and with proper attitudes. God is concerned with our insides, our hearts, for it is from the inside that right behaviour flows (Mark 7:21–23).

So, in 15:7–8, the Israelite must have a generous and selfless heart, full of love for one's neighbour, especially a needy neighbour. This is opposed to being "hard-hearted." The right internal attitude will then result in the right action of "lending enough to meet the need." So right action without the right attitude, that is for the wrong reasons, is not enough. Nor is the right attitude without action. What fulfils this law is a combination of right attitude and right action.

These principles are further underlined in verses 9–11. The Israelite is commanded not to "entertain a mean thought" and not to "view your neighbour with hostility." Rather the right attitude of generosity is to result in giving "liberally" and being "ungrudging." The background here is the Sabbatical (seventh) year remission of debts law (see 15:1–6). At every seventh year, all debts were cancelled out. This law, radical by our standards, aimed to prevent chronic poverty. The temptation was that close to the seventh year a person might be disinclined to lend because the time remaining to recoup the amount lent was small and thus the chances of repayment were limited. That temptation is addressed in verse 9.

The New Testament supports the basic attitudes espoused here. Notably we read in 2 Corinthians 9:7: "Each of you must give as you have made up your mind, not reluctantly or under compulsion, for God loves a cheerful giver." Christian ethics is largely an ethic of gratitude and thankfulness to God. His generosity to his people in Christ should be the main stimulus to our generosity in return. God's generosity is a key theme in Deuteronomy. Blessing and abundance in the land are the focus of this. We saw in the last chapter that God's generosity in productivity and fertility should result in Israel's generous offerings of tithes and firstfruits and care of the landless. In 15:4, the expectation of God's blessing is linked with the suggestion that there need be no poor in the land because God provides enough for all.

Law and Sin

This raises an important supposition of the laws in Deuteronomy. In 15:11 there is an acknowledgement that there will always be poor and needy in the land. Verse 4, which suggested the possibility of there being no poor or needy, is tied to the obedience of the people. Therefore the concession of verse 11 is in effect a recognition that Israel will not be able fully to obey. The two verses together concede Israel's essential sinfulness. Despite both God's generosity and the laws to prevent poverty through unequal distribution, Israel will fail. Its heart is not right.

Many other laws presuppose the same state. So laws, for example, dealing with punishment for adultery and murder presuppose the failure of Israel to keep the Ten Commandments. Thus while some laws state the ideal (e.g. you shall not murder), others are about response to failure or sin and control of sin from spreading. The laws are therefore both idealistic and realistic. Underneath them is an acknowledgement of the sinful nature of Israel. This observation is also reflected in the relationship between the Ten Commandments and the remainder of the laws in Deuteronomy.[1] The Ten Commandments are the idealistic base, the statement of God's absolute standards. The detailed laws which follow demonstrate the realistic working out of these laws. They reflect the expectation that Israel will fail and they show how such failure will be dealt with.

Another way of expressing this is by the distinction between what are called apodictic and casuistic laws. The former are like the Ten Commandments, an absolute statement, "You shall not . . ." Casuistic laws are typically expressed as "If . . ., then . . ." laws. If somebody commits a crime or transgression, then certain action must be taken. Apodictic laws reflect an absolute standard; casuistic laws acknowledge that such a standard will be broken.

Law and God

Another principle suggested by this passage is that of the imitation of God. God is generous and therefore his people should be generous also. This is an important biblical principle, more fully worked out in the New Testament in

---

1. As noted earlier, scholars have often tried to make sense of the arrangement and organization of the laws in Deuteronomy. Many attempts to base this on the Ten Commandments have been made. There appears some validity in seeing Deuteronomy 12–26 as, in general, following the order of the Ten Commandments, but the pattern is not rigid.

terms of the imitation of Christ (1 Cor 11:1; Rom 13:14; Eph 4:32; Phil 2:5; etc.). Its roots lie in the Old Testament. Not only generosity, but truthfulness, faithfulness and love are characteristics of God which he expects of his people. Perhaps the key demand of Israel in Deuteronomy is that of love. God loves Israel and loved its forefathers (4:37; 7:8–9, 12–13; 10:15; 23:5); Israel is to love God (6:5; 10:12; 11:1, 13, 22; 19:9; 30:6, 16, 20). Because God loves the stranger or alien, so ought Israel to do the same, especially because Israel was itself alien in Egypt and God brought Israel out from there (10:12–19). God's care for the widow and orphan (10:18) is later demanded of Israel (14:29). As God shows no partiality and accepts no bribe (10:17), so Israel and its judges ought not accept any bribe (16:19). God's treatment of Israel when it was enslaved in Egypt is the model for how Israel is to treat its slaves (15:15). Many other examples could be found which show that Israel is to reflect the character of God and imitate that character.

Related to this principle of imitation of God is that many of the commandments are grounded in God's redemption of Israel in the past. This illustrates the point made above about biblical ethics being an ethic of gratitude and thankfulness. Since God has taken the initiative in establishing a relationship with Israel through redeeming it from Egypt, the commandments and obedience to them are a matter of response to God's action. So the prohibitions against idolatry throughout the book are grounded in God's revelation at Sinai, as we saw in chapter 4. The Ten Commandments themselves begin with a statement of God's redemption (5:6). The offering of firstlings from flock or herd is a response to God's blessing (15:19–23). Keeping the Passover is to be a response to God's redemption of Israel from Egypt. The ceremony in 26:1–11 is a response to the entry of the land and the enjoyment of its produce. All of this reminds us that the laws are God-centred. They are grounded in the character and action of God. Hence obedience is characterized by imitation of that character, and grateful response to that action.

This is also borne out by the importance of memory in Deuteronomy. Many times Israel is urged to remember such things as its servitude in Egypt (16:12; 24:22); its deliverance from Egypt (5:15; 6:12; 7:18f; 8:14; 15:15; 16:3; 24:18); the covenant made at Horeb (4:9–13, 23); Yahweh himself (4:39–40; 6:6; 8:11, 14, 18, 19; 11:18; 26:13); the wilderness experiences (8:2, 14–16; 9:7; 24:9); Amalek (25:17–19); and the days of old (32:7).[2] To remember is

---

2. E. P. Blair, "An Appeal to Remembrance," *Interpretation* 15 [1961]: 45.

not merely to exercise psychological or intellectual recall but ought to lead to obedience. To forget is to disobey; to remember is to obey. This shows a further link between obedience and God.

One qualifier needs to be made at this point about Israel's obedience as being a grateful response to God. Another dimension is also important in Deuteronomy, namely the promise of future blessing. Much of the motivation for obedience in Deuteronomy is that God will respond to obedience with future blessing. Deuteronomy 28:1–14 sums this up, promising blessings of long life in the land, prosperity and freedom from enemies.

> If you will only obey the Lord your God, by diligently observing all his commandments that I am commanding you today, the Lord your God will set you high above all the nations of the earth; all these blessings shall come upon you and overtake you, if you obey the Lord your God. (28:1–2)

Such promises or motivations also apply in individual cases. The third year tithes are to be offered with the motivation "so that the Lord your God may bless you in all the work that you undertake" (14:29). At one level offering tithes is out of gratitude for God's past action. At another level further, future blessing is also promised. The sequence then is that God freely establishes a relationship with Israel by his grace. He calls Israel to a thankful response of obedience. He, in turn, will bring further blessing as a response to Israel's obedience. Similarly, the command to lend to the needy is motivated by a promise of blessing, "then because of this the Lord your God will bless you in all your work and in everything you put your hand to" (15:10). Likewise, the law regarding the Feast of Tabernacles, "For the Lord your God will bless you in all your harvest and in all the work of your hands, and your joy will be complete" (16:15). This future-oriented motivation is sometimes expressed as a warning, often introduced by "lest" (e.g. 7:25; 8:12; 19:6; 20:5–8; 22:9; 25:3). These warn Israel against a particular course of action because God will bring about an undesirable action as a consequence.

Chris Wright sums up the relationship between obedience and God, which we have been discussing, under four headings: God-centred origin, meaning that God acts first and then Israel responds; God-centred history, meaning that because of what God has done in the past and what he will do in the future, what Israel does now has meaning and will be grounded in God's action; God-centred content, meaning the imitation of God's character; and God-centred motivation, meaning gratitude, memory and personal experience of what God has personally done for Israel should be a motivation for its obedience.[3]

Mutual Responsibility

Another important principle which the laws reveal is that of personal responsibility. For many people, their conception of what God requires is expressed in terms of not doing harm to anyone else. The laws in Deuteronomy show that God requires something much more positive – a mutual responsibility for each other. Relationship within a community, whether society in general or the fellowship of God's people in particular, obligates each individual to a responsibility for others. Apathy and inaction are not good enough. This is illustrated in a variety of ways.

In 21:1–9, the situation is where,

> in the land that the Lord your God is giving to you to possess,
> a body is found lying in open country, and it is not known who
> struck the person down . . . (21:1)

The murderer is unknown. This law details that the elders of the nearest town shall take responsibility for a ceremony in order to absolve the land from guilt, even though they were innocent of the murder. The principle underlying this is that one person's behaviour affects other people. No person is an autonomous individual. The prayer of the elders is to be, "do not let the guilt of innocent blood remain in the midst of your people Israel" (v. 8).

In a similar sense, 22:1 states: "You shall not watch your neighbour's ox or sheep straying away and ignore them; you shall take them back to their owner." Likewise 22:4, "You shall not see your neighbour's donkey or ox fallen on the road and ignore it; you shall help to lift it up." This principle of responsibility is important. It forces people to act and not be indifferent or apathetic. It reminds us that sin is not just wrongdoing, sins of commission, but that sin can be not doing anything, sins of omission. Apathy, a mark of so much of modern society, is a symptom of lack of relational responsibility, a symptom of selfishness and a symptom, then, of social breakdown. While Christians do not live in a theocratic society (where the ruler of the nation is God, not a king or parliament) as the nation of Israel was intended to

---

3. Christopher J. H. Wright, *Living as the People of God: The Relevance of Old Testament Ethics* (Leicester: IVP, 1983), 21–32.

be, nonetheless relationships, whether with other Christians or with our neighbours of society, bring an obligation of responsibility.

The parable of the Good Samaritan reminds us that this principle is reinforced by Jesus himself (Luke 10:25–37). There is much in our society which discourages taking responsibility for other people. Urban anonymity means those who live in cities are less likely to know their neighbours than in earlier times. Taking responsibility for others is costly. In 22:1–4, the action demanded of the Israelite who finds his neighbour's animal may have been extremely costly, both in time and money. The situation in 22:4, helping a laden animal back to its feet, may well have involved unpacking its load, getting the animal up, and then repacking, all a time-consuming activity. Looking after lost animals (22:1–3) would involve housing and feeding them.

In our day, taking responsibility can be dangerous. Perhaps a modern equivalent of 22:1–3 is when we see a car that has broken down at the side of the road. Are we responsible to stop and offer assistance? Admittedly we have breakdown services which alleviate the problems. Nonetheless, we hear of stories where those who have supposedly broken down are merely staging a breakdown in order to steal from kindly people who do stop. Sadly such incidents mean that exercising mutual responsibility for others today is often unsafe and risky, further encouraging the breakdown of mutual responsibility. Yet of all people, Christians should be willing to risk their own safety for the sake of someone else. Deuteronomy 22:1–4 urges us to exercise that responsibility.

The principle of mutual responsibility is backed-up by the observation that the laws in Deuteronomy are about relationships. They are addressed to a community, not to the individual, and involve relationships within that community, not an individual's isolated behaviour. So God's people are to be a body in solidarity. The sin of one member affects others. Hence, in 21:1–9 above, one town must make an offering to absolve the guilt of murder. Otherwise that sin will "remain in the midst of your people Israel" (v. 8). The prayer is for the absolution of all Israel, not for the murderer alone.[4] Thus the people will "purge the guilt of innocent blood from your midst" (v. 9).

This expression of purging evil or sin or innocent blood occurs a number of times in Deuteronomy (13:5; 17:7; 19:13, 19; 21:9, 21; 22:21). For example, in 19:11–13, the murderer must be executed because the guilt needs to be purged from Israel in order that it may go well with the whole people. In

---

4. See R. Brown, *The Message of Deuteronomy* (BST; Leicester: IVP, 1993) 204–205.

21:1–9, the sin of one person needs dealing with, even though that person is not identified. Otherwise the guilt will remain in the nation. This principle suggests a solidarity of the people in sin and a recognition that sin untreated and unatoned will spread and take hold. Hence it is each person's responsibility to ensure a solidarity free from the contamination of sin.

In 13:6–11, the sin of one person is to be punished severely so that it does not spread to others and they are deterred from committing such a sin (v. 11). The spread of sin from an individual to the nation is also threatened in 29:18–28. The metaphor used there is of a root producing poison which spreads to the rest of the tree, bringing about its downfall. This metaphor shows the link between the individual and the community. So, throughout Deuteronomy, severe punishment must be meted out on wrongdoers, partly as a deterrent (e.g. 17:13), recognizing that untreated sin will spread. Israelites have a mutual responsibility for each other.

This is a challenge for the church today. Many Christians regard their faith and behaviour as private, something that is not anyone else's business. That is not a biblical perspective. If we are Christians, we belong to the body of Christ and hence to each other. Our sin and failure affects other Christians. It is not a private matter; personal, yes, but not private. We need to take more seriously our mutual encouragement by provoking and stirring one another up to love and good works (Heb 10:25).

Law and Life

The laws of Deuteronomy are all-embracing. No part of our life falls outside the scope of God's law. There is no separation or dichotomy between our religious or Christian life and normal or secular life in Deuteronomy. There is only one life and all of it is to be lived in response to and relationship with God. The sheer variety of laws in chapters 22 to 25 in particular bear this out. There are laws relating to lost property, clothing, birds' nests, house roofs, sowing seed, tassels on cloaks, sexual practices, health and hygiene requirements, charging interest, vows, plucking grain, marriage, the newly married, taking millstones as pledges, kidnap, leprosy, payment of wages, reaping a harvest, litigation, fights and dishonest weights, among other laws.

Living as a person of God is, in both Old and New Testaments, a full-time business. No part of life is exempt from the scrutiny of God. After all, the summary of the law did say that Israel was to love with all the heart and all the soul and with all the mind. Nothing was to be left for loving anything else. Again this is a challenge to modern thinking which divides our lives into religious and non-religious compartments. As Christians, our relationship to God should affect everything we do, think and say.

Law, Land and Economic Irrationalism

The land is of great significance in Deuteronomy. As we have seen, it is the main promise of God mentioned in the book and is, therefore, a divine gift. The entry and conquest of the land are immediate tasks facing Israel in Deuteronomy. The laws of Deuteronomy are set in the context of living in the land. The hope of Deuteronomy is for the people of Israel to live under God's law, receiving his blessing, in the land.

As we saw in chapter 3, Israel is utterly dependent on God. The land and all prosperity, wealth and blessing come from God (e.g. 8:17–18). The land is a good land, abounding in everything Israel needs, flowing in milk and honey and described in paradise type terms (6:10–11; 8:7–9; 11:8–12). So 26:5–10 anticipates Israel's arrival in the land and reception of its bounty as it offers the firstfruits to God.

One of the principles of many of the laws is that there is enough in the land for all, provided the Israelites share the produce of the land with each other. So in the laws concerning worship at the central place, offerings and tithes and celebration, explicit mention is made of those who are landless, that is slaves, orphans, widows, Levites and sojourners (e.g. 12:12, 18–19; 14:29; 16:11, 14; 26:12–13). They were to be provided for by those who owned land and had the resources of the bounty of the land. This concern for the underprivileged continues in other laws. "You shall not deprive a resident alien or an orphan of justice; you shall not take a widow's garment in pledge" (24:17; see also 27:19). When Israelites reaped the harvest from their fields, they were not to take up every last piece of grain. If a sheaf of wheat is forgotten, "you shall not go back to get it; it shall be left for the alien, the orphan, and the widow" (24:19). A later illustration of this principle at work is found in Ruth 2 where Ruth gleans the leftovers of the harvest. The same principle is applied to the olive and grape harvests (24:20–21). God provides plenty for all, provided Israelites share with each other.

This principle undergirds laws preventing poverty. We have already looked briefly at 15:1–11. Debts, from one Israelite to another, were to be remitted each seventh year (v. 1). Part of the aim was the prevention of chronic poverty, allowing Israelites the opportunity to start again economically.

The promise of verse 4, "There will, however, be no one in need among you," is a promise consequent on obedience to the law of remitting debts. Open-handed generosity is commanded (vv. 7–8). Slaves are to be liberated every seventh year and provided for liberally (vv. 12–14). Again a promise of blessing is attached as motivation to keep this law (v. 18). This passage is making a striking statement about wealth. Prosperity is not the result of economic rationalism but rather of obedience to God. Wealth and prosperity is a corporate goal, not an individual goal.

The same sort of point can be made regarding offerings, tithes and firstfruits. What is offered to God is not the surplus but the best. It is the priority, not an after-thought. Never are such offerings to be made from the surplus, that is after saving enough for the future. Rather, by making such offerings to God, Israel "may learn to fear the Lord your God always" (14:23). The idea is that by giving, Israel exercises trust in a gracious God who will continue to provide for all its needs abundantly.

All of this is a far cry from the economic pursuits of modern times. The accumulation of wealth has become an all-consuming passion for individuals, companies, and governments alike. There is a warning here. True wealth and prosperity are the fruit of obedient lives. Morality cannot be separated from economics. Sadly there is a growing lack of care and concern for underprivileged people in our society. The elderly, children and the poor are regarded too often as economically unviable. We ignore them to our peril. Economic systems are a theological concern. Our society is driven by the goals of self-sufficiency and economic success, goals opposed to those of Deuteronomy where dependency on a providing God and moral success are paramount. The concern for economics in Deuteronomy should force Christians to consider issues such as wage rates, strikes, social benefit schemes and interest rates (see 23:19–20) theologically. There are implications here for how we vote, not seeking to install the party which promises us the most in our pockets, but rather that which best upholds the moral values and priorities of God – concern for the poor, sharing the bounty of the land, providing ways to avoid chronic poverty.[5]

The blessing of prosperity in the land is conditional upon Israel's obedience to the laws. The curses of Deuteronomy 28:15–68 show that disobedience

---

5. T. W. Mann, *Deuteronomy* (WBC; Louisville: Westminster John Knox Press, 1996), 117–120.

will bring famine and drought and, ultimately, loss of land. Thus there is the motivation here that if Israel obeys, there will be plenty for all.

Deuteronomy's Laws and Today

For many Christians there is an ambivalence, at best, about Old Testament laws. Are they not outdated and irrelevant, no longer binding on us? Sometimes the argument for this position is cultural: we live in different, more enlightened times and these laws apply to primitive cultures only. Other times the argument is theological: that Christians are bound by the New Testament which supersedes the Old. Either way the result is the same. Old Testament laws are ignored.

For those who argue on theological grounds, the only Old Testament laws which remain valid are those which are reinforced in the New Testament. So, for example, Jesus in the Sermon on the Mount reinforces the prohibitions on adultery and murder. These would remain binding on Christians today. In effect this approach ignores the Old Testament entirely. Those who argue on cultural grounds may well dismiss the New Testament laws as well, on the same grounds that they are culturally outdated.

A second approach to Old Testament laws accepts them as binding apart from those the New Testament specifically rejects. So, for example, the laws of sacrifice are superseded by the death of Jesus and the food laws are rejected because Jesus declares all foods clean.

A third approach divides Old Testament laws into ceremonial, civil and moral categories. The first is rejected because of Jesus' death and the second because of the end of the Old Testament nation of Israel. One of the problems with this approach is that the Old Testament itself does not recognize those categories. The Ten Commandments, for example, are usually regarded as moral. Where does the Sabbath law fit? The prohibitions against idolatry are ceremonial and yet no one advocates that idolatry is now permissible. The law prohibiting murder may be moral but what about the punishment for murderers? Isn't that a civil issue? Deuteronomy's laws are all moral because they are all to do with God. God is God over all of life. Some laws combine civil, ceremonial and moral aspects. Such a division is artificial.

The method we adopt for dealing with Old Testament laws seeks to distinguish between theological or ethical principle and the particular or cultural expression of that principle. Let me elaborate. The rejection of many Old Testament laws on the grounds that they are culturally irrelevant throws out the baby with the bath water. All Old Testament laws reflect a theological or ethical principle. Most also reflect a particular culture or historical situation of ancient Israel. For example, in Deuteronomy 22:1–3, as discussed above, the law urges Israelites to care for neighbours' lost oxen, sheep or donkeys. Just because most of us live in an urban culture with cars instead of animals does not mean this law ought to be thrown out. The principle behind the law is that of caring for neighbours' property, exercising mutual responsibility, and so on. That principle, if applied to today, would mean caring for those whose car breaks down, looking after lost dogs perhaps, being involved with Neighbourhood Watch, and so on. The principle gets reapplied to our own culture.

A second step is often needed. The principle identified in the law needs to be traced through the New Testament, in particular through the cross. Some principles will be discontinued (e.g. the geographical distinction of the people of Israel from other nations, a principle which underlies the food laws); others will be continued (e.g. caring for neighbours and their property, as evidenced in the parable of the Good Samaritan, a principle based on the unchanging character of God himself); others will be modified (e.g. the inheritance for the people of God in the Old Testament is the geographical land of Canaan whereas in the New Testament it is a heavenly inheritance [1 Pet 1:4]).

In Deuteronomy there is a consistent rejection of Canaanite idolatry. This is evident, for example, in the command to smash down their altars and poles (12:2–3) and, probably, in the prohibition of boiling a kid in its mother's milk (14:21). I doubt many of us encounter Canaanite idolatry on a regular basis; there are not many Asherah poles around these days. Yet the prohibition against idolatry remains strong in the New Testament also (e.g. 1 John 5:21). Our concern as Christians is not to seek out Canaanite shrines to dismantle them (we probably won't find any), rather it is to shun and avoid any contemporary idolatry, which may be more subtle than in Canaan. If the prohibition about the kid in its mother's milk was anti-idolatry, we probably do not need to have stringent kosher food laws. The principle is idolatry, not kids' mothers. What food is offered to idols in our day and age? That should be our concern.

If I were to make a diagram of this method, it would be as follows:

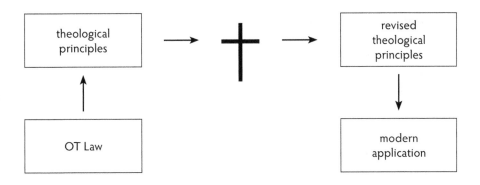

One of the most contentious issues in the church today is sexual morality. Deuteronomy is not silent on this issue and a series of laws relating to sexual relationships occurs in 22:13–30. Like all the laws in Deuteronomy this is not intended to be an exhaustive list. Further sexual laws are found elsewhere in the Old Testament. Like many of the laws in Deuteronomy, it is an elaboration of one of the Ten Commandments, in this case, that prohibiting adultery. Adultery is an infringement of marriage; marriage is a creation ordinance in the Old Testament and an institution or relationship which is intended to parallel that of God for his people as various prophets, not to mention Paul in Ephesians 5, argue. Undergirding these laws, then, is the unchanging character of God and his creation purposes for humanity. No doubt these laws are applied in Deuteronomy to a particular culture – one which does reflect a patriarchal character.[6] Nonetheless Deuteronomy's laws are not one-sided. The law in 22:13–21 protected vulnerable women, guarding their good name (vv. 14, 19) and providing for their future security in the event of divorce. In verses 25–27, the woman is given the benefit of the doubt if raped in the country. In verse 29, while at one level this may look unfair for a young woman, the obligation placed on the man to marry her and never to divorce her offers the woman a security which she may not easily have found as she would no longer have been a virgin.

---

6. Christians disagree over whether the patriarchal nature of the culture of ancient Israel is itself a theological principle or whether God accommodates his laws to that cultural expression. Distinguishing between culture and theology is not always obvious or easy.

Law and Leaders (16:18–18:22)

The laws in Deuteronomy 16:18–18:22 deal with the leadership of the nation, specifically judges, kings, priests and prophets. Leaders above all people were to reflect the character of God.

Judges were to exercise exemplary moral character.

> You shall appoint judges and officials throughout your tribes, in all your towns that the Lord your God is giving you, and they shall render just decisions for the people. You must not distort justice; you must not show partiality; and you must not accept bribes, for a bribe blinds the eyes of the wise and subverts the cause of those who are in the right. Justice, and only justice, you shall pursue, so that you may live and occupy the land that the Lord your God is giving you. (16:18–20; compare 10:17)

Judges were probably local elders, maybe elected from the senior men. In 17:2–7 there is a sample case of a thorough investigation with a public trial (17:4–5). The testimony of at least two witnesses was needed for a case (v. 6). The city gate (v. 5) was the location for business transactions and legal matters (e.g. Ruth 4:1; Amos 5:10). A central court dealt with difficult cases (vv. 8–13). This was to be at "the place which the Lord your God will choose," showing the union between religious and judicial spheres of civil life.

The king is dealt with in 17:14–20, though it was up to four hundred years before Israel had a king. This paragraph establishes the standard by which the subsequent kings of both Israel and Judah were to be judged. Israel was commanded,

> you may indeed set over you a king whom the Lord your God will choose. One of your own community you may set as king over you; you are not permitted to put a foreigner over you, who is not of your own community. (17:15)

So the king is to be like any other Israelite, one of their own community (also v. 20). Again, the moral character of the king was critical. He was to be a model for every Israelite, living under the law. So the king

> must not acquire many horses for himself, or return the people to Egypt in order to acquire more horses, since the Lord has said to you, "You must never return that way again." And he must not acquire many wives for himself, or else his heart will turn away; also silver and gold he must not acquire in great quantity

for himself. When he has taken the throne of his kingdom, he shall have a copy of this law written for him in the presence of the levitical priests. It shall remain with him and he shall read in it all the days of his life. (17:16–19)

Even though a dynastic monarchy is anticipated (v. 20), this is conditional on obedience to the law.

The priestly tribe of Levi was different from the other tribes. Levites lived among the other tribes in forty-eight cities set apart for them (Num 35:1–8; Josh 21). They were supported by tithes, firstfruit offerings, portions of sacrifices not burned on the altar and various gifts of the remainder of the people (18:3–4). Levites ministered in the cities in which they lived, presumably not involving sacrifices, as well as at the central shrine. Possibly there was a roster system for Levites to go to the central shrine to minister there or else they were free to move around (18:6–8).

The final category of leadership was the prophet (18:9–22). Verses 9–14 prohibit a variety of pagan practices, many of which are growing in popularity and influence today, and by which other nations would attempt to discover God's purposes or guidance or determine the future.

No one shall be found among you who makes a son or daughter pass through fire, or who practises divination, or is a soothsayer, or an augur, or a sorcerer, or one who casts spells, or who consults ghosts or spirits, or who seeks oracles from the dead. (18:10–11).

In sharp contrast to these "abhorrent" practices, the prophet whom God will raise up will speak God's word. Israel was to "heed such a prophet" (v. 15). The prophet's role is likened to that of Moses at Sinai (vv. 15–16). This passage promises that God will provide a prophet to fulfil the function for which other nations turn to soothsayers and occult practices. This is an important theological point. God is a revealing God who has provided and will provide the means for his people to understand his purposes and will.

Each of these leaders was bound by the authority of the law. All Israel was to live under God's law, to know it, to learn it, to teach it to their children, to recite it, to hear it being read and to heed it. So too the leaders of the nation were all religious leaders. All were to model living under the law of God.

Throughout all the laws in Deuteronomy, it is clear that the best life is an obedient life. There is indeed no other way.

Questions for Discussion: Deuteronomy 12–26

1) Can you think of things you have done recently which may have been the right action yet you have acted begrudgingly, reluctantly or without a loving heart? Have you repented of such attitudes?

2) Discuss how you would preach Deuteronomy 15:1–11 in your church. Keep in mind to show the principles of the commands, but also as a preacher the need to suggest concrete action also.

3) What principles lie behind the laws in the following passages and how might they be reapplied to your situation?
   i.   22:8 – building a parapet for a roof.
   ii.   24:6 – taking a mill in pledge (note: the millstone is the means for grinding grain to produce flour for food).
   iii. 24:12–13 – not taking a poor person's garment as a pledge (guarantee) for a loan.
   iv.   24:19 – not collecting forgotten sheaves in the field.
   v.   25:4 – prohibiting the muzzling of an ox while it is treading out grain.

4) What "laws" do Christians practise in your country that reflect a legalistic behaviour and do not consider the principles behind the Old Testament laws? These may be laws about food, clothing, games, Sabbath days, or many other things. As a preacher, how do you direct your people to the principles behind the laws?

5) To what extent, if any, does the section on leadership (16:18–18:22) give models for current church and national leadership? What are the major problems of leadership of the church in your country or region?

6) Discuss the sermons you may have heard or preached on various Old Testament laws. What have been their strengths and weaknesses?

Spend time praying for a greater obedience to God's laws.

6

A Heart for God

It is often thought that the God of the Old Testament has a simple formula for responding to people. Those who do good and obey his commandments, God blesses or rewards. Those who disobey, he punishes or curses. Deuteronomy is sometimes used to support this equation. In particular, chapters 27 and 28, which list the curses and blessings of the covenant, seem to support this. So does the statement in 30:15–20, urging Israel to choose good and not evil, life and not death. The implication is that God accepts those who obey him. There is not much room in this equation for accepting those who fail. The truth of the matter is more subtle.

In the ancient world, treaties were often made between two kings or nations, usually instigated by a king who had threatened another. The powerful king would force a treaty on the threatened one, demanding his loyalty and service. Such treaties would often conclude threatening the weak king and his people with various punishments if they resisted the powerful king's rule. However if they were loyal subjects, promises might be given for a prosperous life and livelihood. Deuteronomy 27 and 28 are similar to those treaties. However, the situation is not so straightforward.

Deuteronomy expects Israel to fail. It is not a case of two equally possible alternatives. Israel will fail. We have seen this reflected earlier in the book. Israel had failed forty years previously when the people failed to respond to the spies' report and enter the land from Kadesh-barnea (1:19–46). Then, in an earlier incident, Israel had made a golden calf at Mount Sinai, an act of gross idolatry. This was reported in Deuteronomy 9 where Moses made plain this was not an isolated incident but just one of many acts of stubbornness, hard-heartedness and rebellion (9:6–7, 22–24). The implication there was that the current generation of Israelites is no different from its parents (e.g. 9:6).

Curses and Blessings (27:1–26)

In Deuteronomy 27–28, this expectation is seen in the predominance of curses above blessings. In chapter 28, just fourteen of sixty-eight verses deal with blessings; fifty-four verses deal with curses. In chapter 27, details of a ceremony reciting blessings and curses are given. However only a list of curses follows (27:15–26). This suggests that curses are regarded as the more likely possibility. Israel is expected to fail.

The twelve curses themselves say little that is new. Each begins, "Cursed be anyone who . . ." They refer to practices forbidden elsewhere in the book, though the list itself is diverse. The first two curses (vv. 15–16) refer to two of the Ten Commandments regarding idolatry and honouring parents. Verses 20–23 deal with sexual sin, another link with the Ten Commandments, namely the prohibition of adultery. Verse 24 curses a murderer and verse 25 is also linked to the prohibition on murder. In addition, the other curses refer to property (v. 17) and treatment of the underprivileged and handicapped (vv. 18–19). The final curse is a summary, showing that the infringement of any of the laws in Deuteronomy will result in a curse. The eleven curses are a sample list. There is nothing significant about them, they are just examples.

Perhaps the key point about them is secrecy. The curse on the idolater in verse 15 is on the person who sets his idol or image up "in secret." The same applies to the murderer (v. 24). Earlier in Deuteronomy various forms of punishment are prescribed for those breaking the laws and commandments. The curses address the situation where someone transgresses the commandments but is not detected by other Israelites. The list of curses shows that God still knows. People cannot infringe God's law and get away with it. Other people may not know or detect the sin; but God does.

There is a warning and an encouragement for us here. The warning is that our secret sins, the things we do or think in private, which nobody else knows about, do not go undetected by an all-knowing God. It may be that we think we can get away with such things because nobody else sees. Yet, in the end, we are accountable to God, who does know, even if for the time being he does not act. The encouragement is that God's justice will always prevail in the end. Most of us hate injustice. There is a public outcry if a criminal gets off lightly. Even though human justice is flawed and some transgressors seem to get away with their crimes, these curses encourage us to remember that God is the perfect judge whose justice prevails.

The curses we have been looking at were part of a ceremony to be conducted at Shechem. Shechem is roughly in the centre of the land, in the middle of the area known much later as Samaria. It was the place where God promised Abraham the land (Gen 12:6–7). It was here that Jacob returned with his family (Gen 33:18). It was here that Joseph's bones were taken to be buried (Josh 24:32). What more appropriate place could there be for a covenant renewal ceremony to mark the entry and conquest of the land! The ceremony therefore hints at the faithfulness of God to his promises made to Abraham perhaps six hundred years beforehand.

The ceremony itself was intriguing. Shechem lay on the shoulder of two large hills: Mount Gerizim in the south and Ebal to the north. The tribes were to divide in two.

> When you have crossed over the Jordan, these shall stand on Mount Gerizim for the blessing of the people: Simeon, Levi, Judah, Issachar, Joseph, and Benjamin. And these shall stand on Mount Ebal for the curse: Reuben, Gad, Asher, Zebulun, Dan, and Naphtali. (27:12–13)

Mount Gerizim was the mountain of blessing; Mount Ebal the mountain of curse. It is unclear exactly what the tribes did or said. The Levites declared the curses (v. 14), but presumably this means some priests from within the tribe of Levi who perhaps stood in Shechem, in between the two mountains. The response of "Amen!," made after each of the twelve curses, is said by all the people. Possibly that means all the people on Mount Ebal, the mountain of curse.

The most intriguing thing about the ceremony lies in the instructions in verses 1–8. If I were to choreograph a ceremony like this, I would have a copy of the law and an altar in the centre, in Shechem itself, as a focal point for the ceremony. After all, the law is the basis for the curses and blessings being recited. However, note where these are to be put:

> On the day that you cross over the Jordan into the land that the Lord your God is giving you, you shall set up large stones and cover them with plaster. You shall write on them all the words of this law when you have crossed over, to enter the land that the Lord your God is giving you, a land flowing with milk and honey, as the Lord, the God of your ancestors, promised you. So when you have crossed over the Jordan, you shall set up these stones,

> about which I am commanding you today, on Mount Ebal, and
> you shall cover them with plaster. (27:2–4)

The law, referring to all the laws in Deuteronomy, was to be inscribed on plaster-covered stones which were to be erected on Ebal, not on Gerizim, not in the centre, but on the mountain of curse. Plaster-covered stones were not that unusual in the ancient world though in Egypt where the climate was much drier, the plaster would be long lasting. Such stones would serve as a reminder of the obligations placed on the people. Israel's stones were to be placed on the mountain of curse. Surely the significance of this is that through the law, Israel stands under God's curse. The law, which has described the ideal and perfect standards of God has another function. It exposes sinfulness and failure. In the light of the law of God, Israel's failure is revealed. The law shows up sin.

This is Paul's argument in the New Testament also. He argues in Romans 1–3 that all humanity is sinful and none is perfect. "For 'no human being will be justified in his sight' by deeds prescribed by the law, for through the law comes the knowledge of sin" (Rom 3:20).[1] The same point is made in Galatians 3 where Paul quotes Deuteronomy 27:26: "For all who rely on the works of the law are under a curse; for it is written, 'Cursed is everyone who does not observe and obey all the things written in the book of the law'" (Gal 3:10; similarly 3:19–24).

However there is good news in Deuteronomy 27. The curse is not the final word – otherwise the whole of Deuteronomy would almost be pointless. Next to the plaster-covered stones was to be an altar.

> And you shall build an altar there to the Lord your God, an altar
> of stones on which you have not used an iron tool. You must
> build the altar of the Lord your God of unhewn stones. Then
> offer up burnt offerings on it to the Lord your God. (27:5–6)

The altar was to be made of uncut stones, to ensure it was not like Canaanite altars. This altar was to be for burnt offerings. There were all sorts of sacrifices that Israel had to offer, details of which were given in Leviticus 1–7. Not all were for issues of sin. However the burnt offerings were. "You shall lay your hand on the head of the burnt offering, and it shall be acceptable in your behalf as atonement for you" (Lev 1:4). This is important. Not only does the law expose Israel's sinfulness and show that it stands under God's curse, but

---

1. See also Romans 7:7–25 where the function of the law in exposing sin is also the issue.

God himself provides a way out of that curse through the sacrifice of a burnt offering. The burnt offering sacrifice was an acknowledgement of sin and the means God provided for that sin to be atoned for.

The stones and the altar are a marvellous picture of the heart of God's character. Here is a perfectly holy and just God, whose law reflects his perfect standards and demands. In the light of his holiness, none is perfect. Yet God is also a merciful God, abounding in forgiveness, symbolized here in the altar. God is graciously providing the means for a sinful people to have an ongoing relationship with him. Here on Mount Ebal justice and mercy meet.

The God of the Old Testament is none other than the God of the New. For on the cross of Calvary God's justice and mercy also meet. The New Testament makes it clear that Jesus' death on the cross fulfils what the burnt offerings of the Old Testament herald. There is perfect atonement for sin where "Christ redeemed us from the curse of the law by becoming a curse for us" (Gal 3:13). Rather than leaving us under the curse we deserve because we all fail him, God provides the means for an ongoing relationship with him. This is not based on our obedience or goodness but solely on God's mercy. The simple equation we mentioned at the beginning of this chapter is, therefore, simplistic. It is not simply that God punishes the disobedient and rewards the obedient. None is perfectly obedient but God provides the means for forgiveness and atonement through Jesus, prefigured in the altar for burnt offering.

The final element of the ceremony at Shechem was that after the burnt offering a sacrifice of well-being was to be made, again on Mount Ebal, accompanied by rejoicing. "Make sacrifices of well-being, and eat them there, rejoicing before the Lord your God" (v. 7). It is only after our sin is exposed and atoned for through God's merciful provision that his people can properly rejoice before him.

The pattern of these three things is not unlike the Anglican service of the Lord's Supper. We hear the law, God's standards, expressed through the Bible readings, sermon and the recital of either the Ten Commandments or the two great commandments. The congregation confesses its sin, based on the death of Jesus, and, having been reassured of God's forgiveness, celebrates with a fellowship meal before the Lord with rejoicing.

Both the ceremony at Shechem and the celebration of the Lord's Supper should be times of great rejoicing. Despite all the concerns of life, the troubles and afflictions, doubts and fears, the free, merciful acceptance of us by God through Jesus' death transcends any other aspect of our life. Rejoice we ought; rejoice we must. For what God has done for us in Christ is eternal, unshakeable and done freely for us. What a great God!

The Curses and Israel's History (28:1–68)

This does not mean that Israel's future was rosy. It was not. The curses listed at length in chapter 28 would mostly come to pass. No part of Israel was to be free from God's curse. City and country would be affected, so too both Israel's coming in and going out (vv. 16, 19). These included agricultural problems of plague, famine, drought and affliction of crops and animals. Crops would be planted but there would not be any produce (vv. 38–40). The weather would be affected so that there would not be rain and the earth would turn hard like iron (v. 23). Life would be full of frustration and unfulfilled hopes (v. 30). In addition, Israel would be severely defeated by its enemies who plunder and destroy the land (vv. 25, 36, 48–51). Not only would Israelites be killed, their bodies would be left unburied – a mark of great disrespect – and become food for birds of prey (v. 26). Those who survived would be afflicted with incurable irritable diseases (vv. 27–29, 35, 59–61). Besieged cities would be in such desperate situations that Israelites would turn against each other and even resort to cannibalism in order to survive (vv. 52–57). This is a picture of the most appalling depravity. Some Israelites would be taken into captivity by their conquerors (vv. 41, 64). Yet even in exile, there would be no peace or ease for Israel (vv. 65–68). The description is of unceasing torment.

Could a loving and merciful God inflict such things on his own people? We ought to bear in mind two things. Chapter 28 makes it clear these people deserve such punishment. They have failed to obey God's commandments, a point which is repeated throughout the chapter (vv. 15, 20, 45, 47, 58, 62). They cannot plead ignorance for they have been privileged to have received the laws from God. Second, the wrath of God which is expressed throughout this chapter is not an uncontrollable rage or hot temper. The wrath of God is his holy response to sin. It is part of God's perfect character, an attribute which is not denied but also expressed in the New Testament.

The curses threatened in Deuteronomy 28 came to pass in Israel's subsequent history. After conquering and settling in the land (see the books of Joshua and Judges), Israel became a monarchy (see 1 Sam) and, for a time, a nation of international importance and note. This was under the rule of kings David and Solomon (1000 BC–922 BC; see 2 Sam and 1 Kgs 1–11). However from Solomon's death, the nation's fortunes went downhill. The kingdom divided in two after his death, the northern kingdom being known as Israel and the southern as Judah.

The northern kingdom was marked by a series of bad kings, many assassinations and evil treachery. Perhaps the worst king was Ahab whose wife Jezebel actively opposed the worship of God and set up idols in the country (see 1 Kgs 16–22). Though at times the country was strong politically and militarily, the nation was in terminal decline in the eighth century and was defeated by the Assyrians in 721 (see 2 Kgs 17). This was despite the warnings of the prophets Amos and Hosea a few years before, telling Israel that unless it changed its ways and returned to faithful obedience of God's commandments, defeat would occur. The end of the nation and the threats of Amos and Hosea show the curses of Deuteronomy 28 at work in history. What Moses had warned about centuries before happened. Assyria destroyed the nation, besieged its major cities, and took most of the leading citizens into exile.

The southern kingdom of Judah fared a little better. Some of its kings were good, notably Hezekiah and Josiah. All were descended from David. The nation survived the Assyrian threat which, after Israel's defeat, saw Judah under attack. Despite the siege of Jerusalem in 701 BC under Sennacherib the Assyrian emperor, Jerusalem survived through God's intervention (see 2 Kgs 18–19). The nation lasted another 110 years. The reforms of Josiah were insufficient to change the nation which had plunged into great evil in the reign of Manasseh (see 2 Kgs 21–22). Soon after Josiah's death, Babylon, which had not long beforehand become the dominant nation having defeated and destroyed Assyria, besieged Jerusalem, the second time (587 BC) destroying the city and temple and taking the nation's leaders into exile. Again the curses of Deuteronomy 28 were being realized in history. As the prophets Isaiah, Micah and, later, Jeremiah and Ezekiel had demonstrated, Judah had failed to obey God's commandments and so the strife and defeat which it was suffering was God's punishment on its sin. In many ways the curses of Deuteronomy 28 are the key for interpreting the subsequent history of God's people in the Old Testament.

The Promise of Restoration (30:1–14)

The people of God survived beyond the defeat of Jerusalem and exile, something anticipated by Moses in Deuteronomy 30. Chapter 30 anticipates restoration beyond the period of curse.

> When all these things have happened to you, the blessings and
> the curses that I have set before you, if you call them to mind
> among all the nations where the Lord your God has driven you,
> and return to the Lord your God, and you and your children
> obey him with all your heart and with all your soul, just as I am
> commanding you today, then the Lord your God will restore your
> fortunes and have compassion on you, gathering you again from
> all the peoples among whom the Lord your God has scattered
> you. (30:1–3)

Verse 1 expects an initial time of blessing for Israel, probably referring to the conquest and settlement though also seen later in the highpoints of the reigns of David and Solomon. This is followed by the realization of the curses of chapters 27–28 which we have discussed above. Then after all these things comes restoration. The hope of restoration is initially linked to Israel's repentance after the curses. A key word in 30:1–10 is "return" which occurs seven times in these verses though not always translated the same way.[2] Where Israel is the subject of the verb, the sense is of Israel turning from, or repenting of, its sins which had resulted in the curses. However the future of Israel ultimately does not rest on Israel's change of mind and repentance. It is God who initiates the restoration of Israel's fortunes. This is seen in a number of ways.

Israel's repentance in verse 2 is prompted by God's words being recalled to mind (v. 1). It is God who prompts Israel to turn to him. In a sense, the curses of God on Israel function not only as punishment but also as a call to repent. Also God himself is the subject of the verb "return" in 30:1–10, though that is not obvious in English translations. However the use of the verb with both Israel and God as subject shows a complementary action. God turns to Israel; Israel turns to God. Furthermore, 30:3 states that God "will have compassion on you," referring to his mercy. In Deuteronomy, God's compassion and mercy are tied to his faithfulness in keeping the Abrahamic promises. Though there is no direct reference to the Abrahamic promises in 30:1–10, God's mercy, the land, the metaphor of circumcision in verse 6, the mention of prosperity and multitude of Israelites in verses 5 and 9, as well as reference to the ancestors (literally: "fathers," meaning patriarchs), shows that the restoration of Israel is because God is keeping his promises.

---

2. It occurs in verses 1 (call), 2 (return), twice in 3 (restore, again), 8 (again), 9 (again), 10 (turn). The translation "again" is idiomatic. Literally the expression is "turn to . . . ."

Again we find what we have seen throughout Deuteronomy. Though the book is devoted to exhorting obedience to God's law, in the end it is the grace of God which guarantees the future for God's people. God made promises to Abraham of land, descendants and blessing – promises made unconditionally. That God is keeping those promises, despite Israel's persistent failure and sin, demonstrates his utter faithfulness and reliability. As St Paul says, "Will their faithlessness nullify the faithfulness of God? By no means!" (Rom 3:3–4).

The need for God to show the initiative in restoring Israel lies in the nature of Israel as inherently sinful. This is expressed in 29:4, "But to this day the Lord has not given you a mind to understand, or eyes to see, or ears to hear." The word translated "mind" is literally heart, which in Old Testament thought was the seat, not of the emotions, as much as the intellect, will or mind. It was the most important organ of the person, the centre of their being. This verse is an acknowledgement that Israel's heart was not right before God. Furthermore, despite all the events of the wilderness, which as we saw in Deuteronomy 8 was intended to be a time of testing and discipline, Israel had failed to learn the lesson. Its heart remained unchanged. That is also the thrust of 29:2–8. In verses 2–3 we are told that Israel has "seen all that the Lord did before your eyes in the land of Egypt, to Pharaoh and to all his servants and to all his land, the great trials that your eyes saw, the signs, and those great wonders." Notice the emphasis on seeing. Yet the very next verse says that Israel does not yet have eyes to see. Clearly the contrast is important. Verse 4 refers to a deeper, inner sight, a spiritual acknowledgement of God. Despite all that God has revealed in the previous forty years, Israel does not yet get it right.

Verse 4 reflects an understanding that this spiritual lack on the part of Israel lies beyond its own correction. It is God who will have to rectify the situation, something which he was yet to do as Israel stood poised to enter the land.

This understanding carries over into chapter 30, at the heart of which lies the promise that "the Lord your God will circumcise your heart and the heart of your descendants, so that you will love the Lord your God with all your heart and with all your soul, in order that you may live" (v. 6). The metaphor of circumcision, applied to the heart, is used to indicate the supply of a right heart which was lacking in 29:4. This is something God provides, not something which Israel achieves.

Circumcision was a rite commanded by God for Abraham and all male descendants in Genesis 17. It was a sign of the covenant relationship between Yahweh and Israel. It is an odd sign. Why have a covenant sign that is so private and applies to men only? Perhaps the reason for this lies in the preceding chapter of Genesis. There Abraham has a relationship with his wife's maid, Hagar, which produces a son, Ishmael. Abraham had acted to produce an heir, something which God had promised, but Sarah was barren and the promise had been unfulfilled many years. Abraham took it upon himself to fulfil the promise. This lack of trust in God was countered by God's reassurance of his promises in Genesis 17 and the sign of circumcision. Such a sign therefore was a reminder, at the very place where Abraham failed to trust God, that God was faithful and would keep his promises. Circumcision was a symbol for trusting and obeying Yahweh. Of course it was external. Deuteronomy 30 indicates that it pointed to something internal, the radical circumcision of the heart. After all, it is Israel's heart which is so stubborn, hard and unbelieving (see 9:6; 29:4; etc.).

The circumcised heart is a heart which loves and obeys God (vv. 6, 8). In verses 2 and 10, it seems that Israel's restoration depends on its repentance and obedience. Now we see that its obedience is the product of the change of heart effected by God. In the end it is God who enables Israel to repent and obey and love him. The promise of a circumcised heart lies in the future for Deuteronomy, beyond blessings and curses. To what does it refer?

Similar promises are made by Jeremiah and Ezekiel which, along with Deuteronomy 30, seem to anticipate the fulfilment of this promise in the post-exilic period of Israel's history (Jer 31:31–34; Ezek 36:26–27). After the Babylonians destroyed Jerusalem in 587, Babylon was itself defeated by the Persians in 539. The next year the Persian emperor, Cyrus, issued an edict allowing captives to return to their homelands (see 2 Chr 36; Ezra 1:1–4). However, the return of Israelites was hardly the great restoration anticipated by many. The land was under-populated, depressed and remained a province of Persia without its own king. The people were reluctant to rebuild the temple and only did so after the prompting of the prophets Haggai and Zechariah. In the next century, under the leadership of Ezra the priest and Nehemiah the governor, the walls of Jerusalem were rebuilt and the people renewed their commitment to the law (see the books of Ezra and Nehemiah). Despite all of this, the glory days of David and Solomon were never repeated. The promise of a new or circumcised heart remained unfulfilled.

The New Testament tells us that this promise is fulfilled in the death and resurrection of Jesus and the giving of the Holy Spirit. As Christians are identified in Jesus' death, then their hearts are circumcised. We see this, for example, in Colossians 2:11–14; Romans 2:28–29; Hebrews 8:8–12; 10:16–17. This does not result in immediate obedience as Deuteronomy 30 seems to suggest, but rather a gradual process towards perfect obedience and love. The effects of a circumcised heart are gradual, not instantaneous. Like Deuteronomy, the New Testament recognizes this as an act of God's grace, not something which we deserve or merit.

That Deuteronomy 30 anticipates Christ is also seen in 30:11–14, a passage which Paul quotes in Romans 10 and applies to Jesus Christ (Rom 10:5–10). These verses in Deuteronomy 30, which look somewhat obscure, are simply saying that it is God who enables faithful obedience. Israel does not have to perform a miracle to obey; God does the miracle in making this possible. Paul shows that this is through Christ. Faithful obedience, which Deuteronomy exhorts, is in the end seen to be faith in Christ. Faithful obedience is possible because the word is near, that is in the heart, the heart circumcised by God. Verses 11–14 need to read therefore in the light of the heart circumcised in verse 6.

Choose Life! (30:15–20)

The rhetorical climax of Deuteronomy occurs in 30:15–20. Here the preaching of Moses, exhorting faithful obedience in the land, comes to a head. The chapters which follow are, in a way, appendices to the book. The climax of the book is reached with the injunction or command to choose life.

> I call heaven and earth to witness against you today that I have set before you life and death, blessings and curses. Choose life so that you and your descendants may live, loving the Lord your God, obeying him, and holding fast to him; for that means life to you and length of days, so that you may live in the land that the Lord swore to give to your ancestors, to Abraham, to Isaac, and to Jacob. (30:19–20)

There is a subtlety about the choice being presented which is important. It is not a straightforward case of obey or disobey. We have already seen that Israel, of its own will and strength, will fail. Its sinful nature guarantees that and its heart is yet to be circumcised by God. The choice is between relying on yourself, and thus disobeying and failing, or relying on God's grace. For Israel is exhorted to choose life and life is the result of a circumcised heart, as verse 6 says, "the Lord your God will circumcise your heart . . . in order that you may live." Indeed we can go further. Verse 20 literally says, "for he/it is life to you." Though the original Hebrew could be translated with either "he" or "it," it is unclear what is being referred to. However quite possibly the pronoun should be "he" referring to Yahweh, that is God (compare Deut 32:39). "God is your life" is in effect what Moses is saying. So to choose life is to choose God, for God is the life-giver.[3] Israel is being called to choose God, to rely on his grace, and trust him. Of course obedience is to be part of Israel's response, as verses 16–17 make plain. The obedience which God demands of Israel is faithful obedience, acknowledging that there will be failure but failure that can be forgiven through God's abundant goodness and mercy. The ceremony in chapter 27 underlined this point.

Thus it is God who gives life; Israel does not earn it or deserve it. Life is God's prerogative – that is he is free to give it to whomever he wills. Again we find anticipation of New Testament statements here, most notably Jesus' statements that he is "the life" (John 11:25; 14:6). In addition Jesus is the one who is the bread of life (John 6:35) and the giver of life-giving water (John 7:37–39). The source of life is God himself. Both Deuteronomy and Jesus direct their listeners and readers to that personal source. True life does not exist apart from God. For Deuteronomy, where life is such an important theme throughout the book, to live is to do so in relationship with God and thus to enjoy his blessings in the land. Quality of life is important and without a relationship with God there is no quality in living.

Passing on the Baton (34:1–12)

Moses' life is all but over. This great hero of faith is denied permission to enter the Promised Land about which he had preached so fervently. Within the pages of the Old Testament there is perhaps none so great as Moses. It was he who was called by God in the burning bush to lead God's people from slavery in Egypt through confrontation with Pharaoh. It was he who led Israel through the Red Sea, through forty difficult years in the wilderness to the verge of entry into the land. It was with Moses that God met on Mount Sinai when the Ten Commandments and the rest of the law were given to Israel. Only Moses had met with God face to face. No one else had arisen like him, performed such signs and wonders, or been a prophet like him (34:10–12).

---

3. This is also similar to Deuteronomy 8:3 where life stems from what proceeds out of Yahweh's mouth.

Truly he could be called a "servant of the Lord" (34:5). If anyone deserved to enter the land, Moses did.

Yet Moses, like any other person, had failed God (Deut 1:37; 3:26–27; 32:51). He was not perfect, but he died in faith. He was allowed a panoramic view of the Promised Land from Mount Nebo in modern Jordan. Usually the heat haze makes the view from there limited, so Moses must have had a clear day for he could see the full extent of the Promised Land (Deut 34:1–4). It is clear that God took his life, for Moses was still strong despite being 120 years old (v. 7). The Bible is always realistic about its heroes. No one is perfect, except for Jesus. We need to be careful when using biblical characters as models to follow or avoid. Since none is perfect we cannot always say, "Be like Moses."

However the Bible is ultimately about God, not people. It is God who determines how we should behave. Moses' death looks forward to the fulfilment of God's promises. The land lay before him, a glimpse of the future. This is the pattern of the Bible. Full realization of the promises of God lies in the future. The people of God are always to be looking forward in faith. Yes there are fleeting moments of fulfilment throughout the Bible, but there remains still the promise of rest as the writer of the Hebrews says (Heb 4:9). This is a salutary warning for Christians living in a world demanding instant communication, instant news, instant answers and instant satisfaction and gratification. Not everything God promises is available in full right now. Sadly some Christians make the mistake of claiming too much too soon: perfect health, sinless perfection, perfect joy, a perfect church, perfect peace, and so on. While like Moses we may be privileged to enjoy glimpses of these promises, and see them realized in our lives, complete fulfilment lies in heaven.

The opposite warning also applies. There are many Christians who hold little hope of ever seeing God's promises fulfilled. They have low expectations of God working in the world and accomplishing his purposes in history. Many lack assurance of heaven. Yet Christians are heirs of all the promises of God, the guarantee of which is the Holy Spirit. Christians ought to be marked by hope, a sure and certain hope, for though our inheritance awaits us in heaven, it is an inheritance which is guaranteed for us (1 Pet 1:3–5).

The account of Moses' death focuses in the end not on Moses but on God. For the glimpse of the land that Moses received was God's demonstration of his faithfulness. The land's dimensions are given, showing that this is the land promised to Abraham six hundred years before in Genesis 15. "This is the land of which I swore to Abraham, to Isaac, and to Jacob saying, 'I will give it to your descendants'" (v. 4). Moses could die content because he knew God would keep his promises. He is that sort of God. Deuteronomy began with the promise-keeping God. It ends with the same point. God is faithful. Trust him.

Even if the promises are yet to be realized, trust him, for he is keeping every promise he has made. The real hero is not Moses; it is God.

Since Moses is about to die, provisions are made for the succession of leadership and continuation of the covenant with God. This is the content of chapters 31–33. Joshua is to lead Israel into the Promised Land. He is formally charged with that responsibility by Moses in front of all Israel in 31:1–8. Then, in verses 14–23, Yahweh himself formally commissions Joshua for the task of conquest, entry and leadership. Repeated throughout all these verses, and again in Joshua 1, is the charge to be strong and bold and not to fear. This is not a blanket statement for all Christians in any time or place. The grounds for Joshua not to fear but to be bold are the promises of God – that God is with him in fulfilling his promises of giving land to his people. As Joshua is about the business of obeying God and doing his will, he can rest assured of God's continued presence and assistance and thus must not be afraid. Jesus gives a similar promise and charge to his disciples after his resurrection. His promise to be present with his disciples in Matthew 28:20 is in the context of their obedience in carrying out this Great Commission.

The laws that Moses has given Israel are to remain for all future generations. They do not become obsolete at Moses' death. Measures are therefore taken to ensure they remain in force. Moses writes them down, a reference to the initial writing of the book of Deuteronomy itself (31:9). Every seventh year it was to be read publicly at the Feast of Tabernacles, thus ensuring future generations also heard and learned the law (vv. 10–13). The book was to be deposited in the ark of the covenant, a safe and secure place which would guarantee its preservation (31:9, 24–29). It would act as a witness against a sinful nation in future generations. Sadly, it seems that Israel failed to keep this command to recite and obey all the laws. In the time of Josiah, king of Judah between 640–609 BC, the book of the covenant was found in the temple. Most scholars agree that this was at least part, if not all, of the book of Deuteronomy. It was obviously unknown in his time and its discovery led to further reforms and acts of penitence (see 2 Kgs 22–23).

A further provision for future generations was a song that Moses recited to all Israel, the words of which are kept in Deuteronomy 32. This song was to be another way of reminding future generations of their obligations to God. Significantly it begins with a statement of praise to God, a God who is perfect and faithful (v. 4), the creator of all (v. 8), the sustainer and protector of his people (vv. 10–12). Despite all this, Israel, ironically called Jeshurun, meaning the upright one, turns away from God to idolatry (vv. 15–18), incurring the wrath and punishment of God (vv. 19–38). It is both an outline of Israel's history in the wilderness and a forecast of its future in the land as well. Israel has not learned its lesson from the wilderness.

Finally Moses, like Jacob in Genesis 49, pronounces his blessing on the tribes of Israel. This blessing is another statement of faith in a faithful God. It is a mixture of prayer, praise and warning. It concludes with a statement of praise of the uniqueness of God. We have seen throughout Deuteronomy that idolatry – the worship of other gods – was a serious threat for Israel. So the uniqueness of Yahweh is stressed. "There is none like God, O Jeshurun, who rides through the heavens to your help, majestic through the skies" (33:26). This God has acted for his people in history to save them (v. 29) and protect them (v. 28). He alone is to be worshipped and praised.

Questions for Discussion: Deuteronomy 27–34

1) To what extent does illness, strife, the weather and crop failure represent the curse of God today?

2) Has your heart been circumcised? (30:6) How do you know? What results can you see in your life from having a circumcised heart?

3) Is it unfair that Moses is denied entry into the Promised Land? (consider 32:51).

4) Which attributes of God have been prominent in Deuteronomy? How should each attribute help you in your Christian faith and obedience? Think about your recent sermons. How much have you preached God? How much have you preached human example or law? Is God preached enough in your preaching, the preaching you hear, and in general?

5) What have you learned and reflected on that might change your preaching through this book? How will you put any changes into practice?

Spend time praying for a greater trust in God's faithfulness to his promises. Pray that God helps you preach more faithfully, clearly and relevantly the faithfulness of God and our response of faithful obedience.

Appendix

Preaching Deuteronomy

Deuteronomy combines narrative, as well as law, including a little poetry in chapters 32–33. Each of these types of writing has its own style and issues of interpretation which preachers ought to consider. Overall, Deuteronomy is a sermon, so in many ways the fact that Moses is preaching to Israel makes the task of preaching Deuteronomy today a little easier. Below are some brief pointers to preaching Deuteronomy faithfully, clearly and relevantly. For fuller discussion, see Chris Wright, *Sweeter than Honey* (Carlisle: Langham 2015).

Preaching the Old Testament

When preaching the Old Testament, there are several important points preachers need to keep in mind.

- We need to read the Old Testament through the New Testament, for the New Testament is the continuation of the Old Testament. It is one big story. Further, the bulk of the Old Testament, from Abraham to Malachi, is the start of God's great redemption plan which will be fulfilled by Jesus. So the Old Testament in general is leading us through Jesus to today.
- It is helpful to think of the Bible's story in six stages:
  1) Creation (Genesis 1–2)
  2) Sin (Genesis 3–11)
  3) Redemption Begun (Abraham to Malachi)
  4) Redemption Completed (Gospels)
  5) Redemption Lived and Proclaimed (Acts, Epistles, Revelation 1–20)
  6) New Creation (Revelation 20–21)

- In the category of Redemption Begun, into which Deuteronomy falls, the promises to Abraham are important. The redemption plan is driven by the promises to Abraham of:
  - Descendants
  - Land
  - Blessing
  - Nations being blessed

  These promises find their fulfilment, and development, through Jesus in the New Testament.

- Reading through the New Testament means we need to consider how the themes and issues of the passage we are preaching get developed, or changed, in the New Testament.

- Christians today are not a nation of God's people, but a church scattered through the world. In the New Testament, in the light of the gospel and Jesus, "nation" changes to "church." There is a temptation, when thinking of Israel and its land and nation, simply to jump to our home country today. However, we need to think "church" not "nation" primarily, for it is the church who are the people of God.

- The same issue applies to thinking about land. The Promised Land was part of the Abrahamic promise in the Old Testament. However, the teaching of Jesus, and the epistles, transforms this idea of an earthly promised land into a kingdom not of this world – a kingdom of heaven. So as we consider passages that deal with earthly promised land, we need to think how that applies today to Christians who belong to a heavenly inheritance and land.

- The same applies to blessing. Deuteronomy has been used to promote a prosperity theology of earthly wealth. Those blessings, for example in Deuteronomy 28:1–14, apply to the earthly promised land. Now that the land promise is transformed by Jesus, so is the blessing promise. We have received every spiritual blessing in the heavenly realms (Ephesians 1:3), for example.

- Keep in mind how Deuteronomy shows God keeping those Abrahamic promises, and those promises gradually being fulfilled.

- As we preach the Old Testament, we need to keep thinking and asking, "how does this lead me to Jesus?"

- Remember, the Old Testament is the gospel beforehand. It is the same God, acting for same universal purpose, who saves a people and calls them to holiness for his glory. The Old Testament still speaks today. It is not made redundant through Jesus.

Preaching Old Testament Law

On page 79 in chapter 5, there is a diagram of the process of applying Old Testament laws to today. Use that diagram as you think through preaching Old Testament laws. Some points worth considering:

- One big danger of preaching law is to be legalistic. This book has attempted to show you how Moses preaches God, to stir up faithful obedience, and to show how faith and obedience go together. So as you preach on a law passage, make sure you keep people's attention on God, his character and action for us, to stir up obedience. Don't separate the law from the grace of the gospel or you become legalistic.
- Think carefully how to give some specific and concrete examples of putting the principles into practice. Don't simply preach an abstract application, like "love your neighbour" or "be generous." Help people think how to put those principles into action. However, at the same time, preachers need to be careful that the examples they use do not create a new law. So you need to consider carefully whether this concrete application applies to all Christians all the time or is it for some people. For example, if the principle is being generous, giving $100 may not be the right concrete application for everyone. If the principle is respect of elders, how we practise that will vary from culture to culture, person to person.
- As you preach through Deuteronomy's laws, keep going back to God's faithfulness and rescue of Israel in chapters 1–4, and even the preface to the Ten Commandments. Keep reminding people of this grace context within Deuteronomy itself.
- Look at the reasons for obedience scattered through Deuteronomy. Apart from thankfulness for God's character and rescue, there is also the motivation for future blessing, such as "live long in the land," etc. Obedience will go hand in hand with trusting God's future provision and goodness also. Another motivation is God's desire to bless the nations. So as a preacher, consider how to motivate your people biblically towards faithful obedience.

Preaching Old Testament Narrative

Part of Deuteronomy is narrative, namely chapters 1–3, 9, and 34. When preaching narrative, a few things are important to remember:

- Keep thinking about what God is doing in this narrative. Don't use narratives simply as moral lessons, or examples to follow.
- Don't allegorize history. Some preachers might say, for example, the spies were afraid of giants in the land. Who are the giants you are afraid of? That tends to allegorize the history. Try and get underneath the narrative to see the point that Moses is making.
- Don't simply combine the narratives in Deuteronomy with their counterparts in Exodus or Numbers. Rather, compare them, don't combine. What does Deuteronomy highlight by leaving out other things, etc.? That helps us grasp Moses' emphasis as he preaches the narrative. I have tried to show this principle for Deuteronomy 1–3 in chapter 1 of this book.
- Don't add things to the narrative in an attempt to make it more interesting. Rather, highlight in your sermon the tension, plot, and excitement in the narrative itself.
- Keep in mind two things: the event that happened in history, but also why that historical event is being told in this way. When we tell someone what happened in our life, we shape how we tell them depending on who they are and what we think they are interested in. That is what Moses does in Deuteronomy. These narratives are not simply history lessons, but narrating history for a purpose.

Preaching Deuteronomy

Deuteronomy is a long book, and a sermon series through every verse and passage may become too long for many churches and congregations. How can you preach the book?

- One way is to give a sermon series of selected chapters from the entire book so your congregation has a sense of the whole. For example, chapters 1, 4, 5, 6, 9, 12, 15, 16, 18, 26, 28, 30, 32, and 34 (or parts of those chapters).
- Another way is to take a series through Deuteronomy 1–11, maybe have a break and preach another book for a while, come back to chapters 12–26, and then later a third series through chapters 27–

34. The danger of this approach is that we forget the earlier chapters, so you would need to keep reminding people of the context of what you are preaching.

- As you preach, help people work out for themselves how to apply the laws. Explain the process in the diagram on page 79 in chapter 5, and take people through the steps so they can begin to think for themselves.
- Remember that Deuteronomy makes it clear that people are unable by themselves to keep God's laws. Our hearts fail us. Yet Moses preached, and we must also do so. But do not be discouraged when lives do not change as we expect. We are slow to change and reform. That is why we must preach deeply, to our hearts, and not simply on behaviour only.
- Be encouraged in preaching Deuteronomy that the topics keep changing, each chapter is something new, from worship to food to giving to feasts to leaders, etc. All of life is touched through the laws. In a way, therefore, preaching Deuteronomy will challenge people deeply, in areas of sin and bad behaviour. But by preaching through a book, we can preach tough ethical issues without looking like we are picking on people. We preach the issues because Deuteronomy deals with them, and they are relevant. So do not avoid the tough issues!

General Comments

- Preaching the Old Testament in many places is hard because of ignorance of the story and events of the Old Testament. Sometimes we need to take time in our sermons to make sure people know the context and background. Don't bore people with details, but help awaken interest in the Old Testament, its relevance and importance to us today.
- Some passages are long, so they take time to read, let alone preach.
- Sometimes we need to do some work to understand the culture, principles and background of the laws or events.
- Preaching the Old Testament, and Deuteronomy, is a glorious privilege. Be faithful, clear and relevant!

Further Reading

There are a number of good commentaries on Deuteronomy at various levels and for various readers. I recommend the following (books with asterisks are especially suitable for beginning preachers):

D. I. Block, *Deuteronomy* (NIVAC; Zondervan, 2012).

> This is one of the great commentaries of any biblical book in my opinion. It is substantial, but is ideal for preachers with very helpful sections to consider how to connect to our world. Written from a Western view, it may not always be directly relevant in the majority world.

*R. Brown, *The Message of Deuteronomy* (BST; IVP, 1993).

> This series seeks to expound the text, applying it to contemporary times and issues, rather than being a verse by verse commentary. This commentary is certainly accessible for general readers.

I. Cairns, *Deuteronomy: Word and Presence* (ITC; Handsel/Eerdmans, 1992).

> This is a stimulating commentary at a basic level and makes many good observations about the book.

P. C. Craigie, *Deuteronomy* (NICOT; Eerdmans, 1976).

> Similar in depth to Merrill, this is an older commentary which remains a standard text. It is at a more advanced level and deals with the Hebrew text in an accessible way.

*J. D. Currid, *Deuteronomy* (Evangelical Press, 2006).

> This commentary is substantial but written for a layperson and does not require knowledge of Hebrew.

*A. Fernando, *Deuteronomy* (Preaching the Word; Crossway, 2012).

> This is a series of expositions through Deuteronomy, ideal for preachers.

T. W. Mann, *Deuteronomy* (WBC; Westminster/John Knox Press, 1996).

> This commentary has good insights and raises useful issues about the book. It also is at a basic level.

J. G. McConville, *Deuteronomy* (AOTC; Apollos, 2002).

> This is an excellent commentary on the text with very engaging and thought-provoking theological comments.

E. H. Merrill, *Deuteronomy* (NAC; Broadman & Holman, 1994).

> This is more thorough and scholarly but remains accessible for preachers and teachers without Hebrew.

P. D. Miller, *Deuteronomy* (Interpretation; Fortress, 1990).

> This stimulating commentary seeks to apply the issues of Deuteronomy to today. It is more an exposition than a verse by verse analysis.

J. A. Thompson, *Deuteronomy* (TOTC; IVP, 1974).

> This remains a standard introductory commentary, concentrating on the meaning of each verse or paragraph.

E. J. Woods, *Deuteronomy* (Tyndale Old Testament Commentary; IVP, 2011)

> This commentary is the new Tyndale one and is very good, at a relatively straightforward level and accessible for those who do not know Hebrew.

*C. J. H. Wright, *Deuteronomy*. NIBC. Peabody/Cumbria: Hendrickson/ Paternoster, 1996.

> This is an excellent commentary suitable for people without much theological training and background.

There are two major, scholarly commentaries from Jewish commentators which are well worthwhile for the serious student:

J. Tigay, *Deuteronomy* (JPS Torah; Jewish Publication Society, 1996). Both are detailed, deal with the Hebrew text and are fine commentaries.

M. Weinfeld, *Deuteronomy 1–11* (AB; Doubleday, 1991)

The best commentary on the Hebrew text remains that of:

S. R. Driver, *Deuteronomy* (ICC; T & T Clark, 1902 [3rd Ed]).

The fullest bibliography of books and articles on Deuteronomy is found in:

D. L. Christensen, *Deuteronomy 1:1–21:9* (WBC; Word, 2001) and

Deuteronomy 21:10–34:12 (WBC; Word, 2002).

Paul Barker has also written *Teaching Deuteronomy* in the Pray, Prepare, Preach series published by The Good Book Company, 2014. This book, and the series, provides sermon outlines and notes in simple English for preachers. The book is currently available in English, French, Burmese and Nepali.

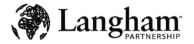 **Langham**
PARTNERSHIP

Langham Literature and its imprints are a ministry of Langham Partnership.

Langham Partnership is a global fellowship working in pursuit of the vision God entrusted to its founder John Stott –

> *to facilitate the growth of the church in maturity and Christ-likeness through raising the standards of biblical preaching and teaching.*

Our vision is to see churches in the majority world equipped for mission and growing to maturity in Christ through the ministry of pastors and leaders who believe, teach and live by the Word of God.

Our mission is to strengthen the ministry of the Word of God through:
* nurturing national movements for biblical preaching
* fostering the creation and distribution of evangelical literature
* enhancing evangelical theological education

especially in countries where churches are under-resourced.

Our ministry

Langham Preaching partners with national leaders to nurture indigenous biblical preaching movements for pastors and lay preachers all around the world. With the support of a team of trainers from many countries, a multi-level programme of seminars provides practical training, and is followed by a programme for training local facilitators. Local preachers' groups and national and regional networks ensure continuity and ongoing development, seeking to build vigorous movements committed to Bible exposition.

Langham Literature provides majority world preachers, scholars and seminary libraries with evangelical books and electronic resources through publishing and distribution, grants and discounts. The programme also fosters the creation of indigenous evangelical books in many languages, through writer's grants, strengthening local evangelical publishing houses, and investment in major regional literature projects, such as one volume Bible commentaries like *The Africa Bible Commentary* and *The South Asia Bible Commentary*.

Langham Scholars provides financial support for evangelical doctoral students from the majority world so that, when they return home, they may train pastors and other Christian leaders with sound, biblical and theological teaching. This programme equips those who equip others. Langham Scholars also works in partnership with majority world seminaries in strengthening evangelical theological education. A growing number of Langham Scholars study in high quality doctoral programmes in the majority world itself. As well as teaching the next generation of pastors, graduated Langham Scholars exercise significant influence through their writing and leadership.

To learn more about Langham Partnership and the work we do visit **langham.org**